Praise for David Taylor's
THE NAKED LEADER

'The business-book bestseller executives are taking on holiday'
Financial Times

'At last – a self help book that is actually helpful'
Computing

'This book makes success within everyone's grasp'
Daily Mirror

'David provides easy-to-learn, proven methods and skills that produce outstanding results . . . If you are into leadership, then you must be into *The Naked Leader*'
René Carayol, co-author of *Corporate Voodoo*

'An extraordinary book for an extraordinary time . . . Compulsory reading for any organisation that believes in the power of a motivated workforce'
Simon La Fosse, Director, Harvey Nash plc

'Drives a stake through the heart of everything consultants have told us for the last twenty years'
David Oliver, CEO Nascent Form

'This is the right book, by the right person, at the right time. It changed my life'
Peter Warman, Chairman Deep-Think

'David has the ability to take the seemingly complex and break it into manageable, understandable and memorable strategies for improvement'
David Butler, Founder and CEO of The Butler Cox Foundation

'The first must-read book of the 21st century, a masterpiece'
Thomas Power, Chairman, Ecademy

'David is the UK's leading light of leadership development'
Michael Gough, Chief Executive, NCC

'At last – the antidote to all those wasted "quality" initiatives; there is another way'
Robin Bloor, C

'A journey of enlightened leadership, lead by the Naked Leader of our time'
Julie Bryant, Creative Director, The Creative Consultancy

'*The Naked Leader* brings fun, adventure and inspiration back into business and personal success'
Adrian Gilpin, Chairman, The Institute of Human Development

'I have bought a copy for my daughters and my whole family – your book is one of the must-read books of all time'
Maurice Spillane, CEO, Appligenics

'*The Naked Leader* does exactly what it says on the "tin"'
Business Plus

'Enlightenment at last – business success through being yourself!'
Dr Alan Rae, Founder, Executive Studio

'Brilliantly written. An antidote to the usual soporific management tomes'
Michael Clarke, Founder, ACTS

'At last! An entertaining business book that really delivers – and about time too!'
Rob Wirszycz, Director, Momentum Capital

'I had been taken hostage by life until I read *The Naked Leader*. It makes pursuing the truth great fun'
Paul Stephenson, CEO and Founder, EGOstream

'*The Naked Leader* uses the most advanced techniques available to transform peple's ideas about life, without once resorting to jargon, mystery or academic double-speak'
Joe Crosbie, Head of Marketing, The Children's Society

'*The Naked Leader* shows us not only how to understand ourselves and what we really want, but also what we need to do to achieve it. I strongly recommend this to anyone who wants to achieve their real potential'
Kris Kebby, Systems Director, Royal and Sun Alliance

'I loved the refreshing honesty and truth of *The Naked Leader* and that it contained practical suggestions which I could apply immediately. And its style is wonderful'
Jeff Skinner, Human Resources Director, 3M

'The most powerful book I have ever read (and I've read a few!)'
Vincenza Douglas, Founder and CEO, Something Beginning with V

'*The Naked Leader* inspires, encourages and enlightens . . . This engages everyone, turning dreams into reality'
Wendy Thorley, Head of Information Systems, RSPCA

'David Taylor is not only a genius, but a brave genius, for daring to stand up and take leadership back to the single issue that really matters: YOU'
Tony Dowd, Project Manager, Aon Consulting

'I have successfully applied the principles of Naked Leadership in both my professional and personal life since reading the book; I'd recommend the book to anybody who wishes to make a difference to their life!'
Paul Heath, Leadership Consultant

'*The Naked Leader* is guaranteed to change the way you think and feel about yourself as a leader'
Robin Harris, IT Director, Smith and Nephew

'David has this incredible ability to energize every individual. He helps you see your dreams are achievable'
Peter Shuttleworth, Head of Service Management, MoD

'What a breath of fresh air in comparison to all the jargon books out there'
Lewis Cunningham, Project Manager, Cornhill Insurance

'At last, a business book that is fun to read, relevant to everybody and truly life-changing'
Jon Bernstein, Silicon.com

the naked leader

NEW REVISED EDITION

david taylor

with best wishes

David

BANTAM BOOKS

LONDON · NEW YORK · TORONTO · SYDNEY · AUCKLAND

THE NAKED LEADER
A BANTAM BOOK : 0 553 81565 2

Originally published in Great Britain by Capstone Publishing Limited (a Wiley
Company)

PRINTING HISTORY
Capstone edition published 2002
Bantam edition published 2003

3 5 7 9 10 8 6 4

Copyright © David Taylor 2002

The right of David Taylor to be identified as the author of this work has been asserted
in accordance with sections 77 and 78 of the Copyright Designs and Patents Act
1988.

Please visit www.nakedleader.com for details of David's next book, and to join the
Naked Leader Network.

Set in 10½/14pt by
Falcon Oast Graphic Art Ltd.

Bantam Books are published by Transworld Publishers,
61–63 Uxbridge Road, London W5 5SA,
a division of The Random House Group Ltd,
in Australia by Random House Australia (Pty) Ltd,
20 Alfred Street, Milsons Point, Sydney, NSW 2061, Australia,
in New Zealand by Random House New Zealand Ltd,
18 Poland Road, Glenfield, Auckland 10, New Zealand
and in South Africa by Random House (Pty) Ltd,
Endulini, 5a Jubilee Road, Parktown 2193, South Africa.

Printed and bound in Great Britain by
Cox & Wyman Ltd, Reading, Berkshire.

Papers used by Transworld Publishers are natural, recyclable
products made from wood grown in sustainable forests.
The manufacturing processes conform to the environmental
regulations of the country of origin.

www.**books**at**transworld**.co.uk

For Rosalind and all my family, with all my love

The greatest mystery of life, is who we truly are.
Alexandre Dumas

thank you

God, and (in alphabetical order), Douglas Adams, Adam Afriyie, Philip Allen, Mark Allin, David Barker, Jon Bernstein, John Blake, Robin Bloor, Gareth Brown, René Carayol, Stephen Clint, Joe Crosbie, Ken Deeks, Neale Donald Walsch, Paul Downs, Tricia Drakes, Adrian Gilpin, Nicola Hunt, Hugh Macken, Lex McKee, Bill Parslow, Brinley Platts, John Riley, Nigel Risner, Anthony Robbins, Karl Schneider, Charlotte Smith, Colin Turner, Brenda White.

Author's note

Welcome to *The Naked Leader*

Helen Keller said 'life is either a daring adventure, or nothing.' I know what she meant – pulling 25 years of corporate learning, lessons and experience into one book has been an adventure indeed – I have been travelling the ups and downs of the journeys themselves, while I have been writing them.

I would like to thank everyone who helped to make the first edition of this book so successful, Transworld for enabling these powerful messages to now reach a wider audience, and particularly my wife Rosalind, who has stood by me and believed in me every single day during the good times and bad.

With every good wish in all that you do, all that you are, and all that you will be.

David

David (2003)

contents

delivering the dream

Books are very personal, and we will read them as we wish. We will fold over the corners of the page, but scream at others for doing the same. We will scribble in the margins (sometimes in pen), we will write a large NO every now and again.

Quite right too.

Welcome to a very personal book.

This book is yours, and like all books you can read it in any way that you wish. Business authors tell me how upset they get when they hear of their books being read any way other than they intended. Apparently being read backwards is sacrilege, randomly is unforgivable, and not at all is normal, with only 10% of business books being read beyond the first chapter, let alone finished, or actioned on!

As this is my first book, I am probably being very naïve,

but I wanted to make this book as different as everyone reading it, as exciting as life can be, and as personal to you as possible. So, in addition to the many ways you can read any book, I am also providing you with thousands of additional choices.

Success is a very personal and unique experience – yours – and as leaders we are all on different paths, and that is exactly what I have provided.

If you don't like this idea, blame me, and read it any way you wish, if you do like this idea, thanks go to Olivia, my stepdaughter.

The Naked Leader is an adventure, taking you to wherever you want to be. It can be travelled from beginning to end, or joined at any stage.

It is structured around seven journeys, starting with The Structure of Guaranteed Success and ending with, well, you will see.

You can choose to follow your own journey all the way through, or you can switch at any stage to a different journey.

The seven journeys are:

Leadership of . . .

1	Self
2	People
3	Teams
4	Company
5	Culture
6	Skills
7	Career

Each 'inspiration' will be a 500–800 word article, in the following structure:

- where you have come from;
- where you are on your personal journey;
- 500-800 words on the challenge, issue or subject: what it means and exactly what to do to achieve what you want and move on; and
- an inspirational story, person or example.

Each one is stand-alone, and can form part of whatever journey you have chosen.

Why *Naked*? Because it's time to strip away the hype, the jargon and complexity that surrounds success. It's time for profound simplicity. And so, each section is totally pragmatic, and written in clear, concise, jargon-free language.

With many options before you, welcome to *The Naked Leader*, and to Naked Leadership.

the structure of guaranteed success

Imagine that success has a structure. Imagine it as a formula, and that, if you follow it, you will achieve whatever you dream, desire and deserve. In effect, imagine that success is *guaranteed*.

Guaranteed, no matter what your background, your present position, where you want to go, or who you want to be.

Imagine no more, for your success is indeed guaranteed. It is a formula that, when followed, will lead you wherever you want to go. We cannot forget change, or chance, as they will play a part, however your fundamental driving force, by far, is choice.

Your future, your choice.

Over the last seven years I have been studying every theory, reality and form of leadership, with three aims in mind:

1. To discover if there is a common formula that runs throughout them all.

2. To find out what always works; not to invent something new, indeed, quite the reverse.

3. To remove all the academic jargon, author hype and deliberate mystery, and apply everything that works into day-to-day realities for people like you and me.

And so Naked Leadership was formed – an approach to leadership that strips away the hype, applies the most powerful, proven tools and techniques to real life without any inherent mystery, and gives people back to themselves.

Naked Leadership has seven principles, and the **first** is that success has a structure, it is a formula and, despite everything that we have been told, that formula is very, very simple.

Having read literally hundreds of success, business and leadership books, attended conferences throughout the world, and worked with individuals, teams and organisations, I have found the formula for success is always the same. And this was a confusing discovery, as often this formula has been hidden behind the most amazing jargon, hype and mystery.

The aim of this book is to blow all of that away; so, to start with, here it is – just a few pages in – the formula for success that other books take hundreds of pages to reveal.

The formula for guaranteed success:

1 **Know where you want to go.**

2 **Know where you are now.**

3 **Know what you have to do, to get to where you want to go.**

4 **Do it!**

Silence in your head – enjoy that silence for a few moments, indeed, re-read the formula a few times.

Allow those thoughts from your 'internal judge' that tell you success cannot be that simple.

Welcome those feelings of doubt that you have wasted your money on a weird book.

But even as you have these two streams of thinking, please also invite in a third.

What if I'm right?

What if this formula is right, and that if you follow it, you will achieve anything you want?

What if you have opportunities beyond anything you previously thought possible? The future of your choosing, the life of your dreams?

Imagine if you simply could not fail:

- **What would you do?**
- **Where would you go?**
- **Who would you be?**

For that is the promise that this book delivers.

And what's more, I am not even going to ask you to believe it. Most leadership and human potential books tell you that you have to believe them, for them to 'work'. I am taking the completely opposite view. In fact, I would prefer you not to believe – just go out and do it. Put what is in this book into powerful practice in your life in order to:

- reclaim your life, and your career;
- reignite your relationships and your team; and
- reinvent your organisation.

And so, the first principle of Naked Leadership is that success is a formula. What's more, it is a simple formula. Most success formulas, all the same as this one, made much more complex, are so hard to understand – meaning that you do not have time to achieve your own success, because you have still to work out how to do it!

Not any more, you now have the formula, the big secret has been revealed. And the secret shall set you free! Actually, you have had this formula all of your life, probably not realising it. You will have achieved amazing success in your life already, in many ways, and each and every achievement followed that same structure.

1. Know where you want to go.

2. Know where you are now.

3. Know what you have to do, to get to where you want to go.

4. Do it!

But your 'judge' told you earlier, if the formula is this

simple, why do so few people achieve 'success' by their own standards? Why do so many people seem unhappy with life, why do so many end their time on this earth feeling they wish they could have done, and been, so much more?

This is exactly what I have been studying – not simply *the* formula, but *how* to achieve success by following the formula. To do this I have met with, learned from, and had the great honour to work with some of the most 'successful' organisations in the world. I have spent hundreds of hours with children, I have stood under Oblivion at Alton Towers, in the rain, and I have met with people from all walks of life.

From all of this input (I hesitate to call it 'research' because most research I have ever read is so BORING!) I have identified the specific actions that we must take to navigate this formula.

1. **Know where you want to go – dream bigger dreams, and know when they have been achieved.**

2. **Know where you are now – take ownership of your life, and be honest about where you are.**

3. **Know what you have to do, to get to where you want to go – widen your choices, and make true decisions, closing off all other options.**

4. **Do it! – With a persistent action – persistence is incompatible with failure.**

I am not arrogant enough to suggest this is 'my' formula, it is not. I have simply distilled it down from hundreds of other, more complex success definitions. And so it is not mine to 'give' to you now, nor yours to take. For it is *already* yours, from the moment you were born.

Indeed, this is the **second principle** of Naked Leadership: this formula does not 'belong' to anyone – it belongs to everyone. It belongs to you, it belongs to everyone you know, it belongs to everyone on this earth. A lot of so called 'gurus' have made themselves very rich by pretending that this formula, or more likely a very complex variation of it, belongs to them. They then make you and me, and everyone, reliant on their complex interpretation of this formula, and therefore dependent on them.

Others rush to copy them, and in the mad rush to claim that some are right and others are wrong, everyone falls out with everyone else. The greatest irony about leadership success is the numbers who preach it, but do not live it.

A classic example of this is Neuro-Linguistic Programming (NLP), the science of human potential and, in particular, rapport. Its two founders, Richard Bandler and John Grinder, have not spoken to each other for over five years, and have recently been suing each other through the American courts!

The **third principle** of Naked Leadership is: to be successful, you need rely on no one, other than yourself. Everything you need, to be anything you want, lies waiting and within you.

It is totally natural that we should feel that the 'answers' lie outside of ourselves. After all, that is what we are taught at school ('I am the teacher so I know the answers, you are the student and you are here to learn'). And so it is in life:

I remember when I was 8, looking up at 16-year-olds wishing I could be them, because they must know so much. Then I was 16, looking up to 25-year-olds. The wisdom and happiness they must have! Then I was 25 looking up at 30-year-olds, and then I was 30, looking back at 16-year-olds, wishing I was that age again!

The **fourth principle** of Naked Leadership says that success is whatever you want it to be, it is yours to define. Traditionally we have been taught that success means a certain amount of money. It is, if that works for you. We have been taught that it means a certain social standing. It does, if that works for you. More often, however, I find people think of success in a different way. They talk about their relationships, they talk about love, happiness and inner peace. They look for a greater meaning in being alive, they seek greater levels of fulfilment, perhaps living with higher integrity. Increasingly also, they seek ways of helping others, to make a contribution.

It would be a very boring world indeed it we all had exactly the same definitions of success. And perhaps the 20th century forced us to believe that we can only be successful if we achieve more than other people. Has this made our world a better place? Has this helped you achieve all you seek? As you read this now, are you totally fulfilled in all that you do, and all that you are?

The **fifth principle** of Naked Leadership is that success can happen very fast, often in a heartbeat. Everywhere we are surrounded by change, and we have learned little from the disastrous 'change' initiatives of the late 20th century. Naked Leadership is not about change for its own sake, (although change will be the result). We focus on *choice*.

It is our choice that determines whether we give our best. As human beings we will only do something to the best of our ability for one reason, and one alone, and that is if we want to.

Personal choice is very important. Indeed, the main reason that 'change' initiatives have not delivered all that they promised over the last twenty years, is because people are very, very uncomfortable with change. And it is no good telling people they 'have to embrace change' if you want them to give their best, they will not. If you do not agree that change causes discomfort, and you are a woman, sleep on the other side of the bed tonight (if you sleep alone please do not get confused with this one). If you are a man, give the TV remote control to your partner for a week.

With choice comes decision, and decisions are at the heart of your future. Think about a company or organisation you have worked in. You would have a weekly meeting about management of a team, or strategy, or an open forum, or whatever. You go along one week, and the people present make a decision. The following week you return, and you find that the same subject and 'decision' are being rediscussed. Have you ever had this experience?

Of course you have, most companies thrive on it!

A decision, a true decision, means quite simply, to *close off all other options*. And that is not an easy thing to do, because to move away from where you are at the moment, as a person, a leader, a team or an organisation, may mean leaving something behind you. However, start to make decisions in which you close off all other options, and your life, your projects and your company will be transformed.

Some of you will be thinking, that cannot be done. After

all, we may not have all the information we need to make a decision, or we may choose a particular path to follow, and then new information comes to light and so it is right to return and reconsider. Indeed, when we look back at 'wrong' decisions, we often cite information and knowledge that only became available after that decision was made.

It is entirely your choice.

In my experience, most people use the 'we don't know enough yet' argument to delay making decisions, and that has cost many organisations very dearly, with many going under. Because not making a decision is a choice in itself.

Success is about making true decisions, and moving on to action. We can all look back and say 'with hindsight'. Just remember the ultimate hindsight we look back on. As you are about to leave this earth, will you look back on your life and wish you had started something new, spent more time with your family or been more than what you became, in any way?

When we say that your future is your choice, part of you will feel very, very uncomfortable:

- **because we have removed your excuses;**
- **because we have opened up limitless possibilities – too many to fathom; and**
- **because we are giving you back to yourself.**

But that discomfort is nothing compared to regrets that we can do nothing about, or wishing we had done things differently, or lived a fuller life.

And you can, because you are alive, right here, right now. Alive in the rich tapestry of life. As it says in *Dead Poets Society*:

*'You are here, and life exists, an identity. That the power-
ful play goes on, and you may contribute a verse.* **That the
powerful play goes on, and you may contribute a verse.**
What will your verse be?'

The **sixth principle** of Naked Leadership is that everyone
has value, that everyone can be anything they want, and
that everyone is a leader. Leadership is not about leaders
and followers anymore, it is about leadership from within,
leaders are everywhere. They are all around us.

The idea that leadership is the exclusive domain of a
chosen few who happen to sit at the top of an organisation
chart, or in parliament, has already lost any credibility it
had. You are as much a leader as anyone.

This book is not about the theory of leadership. If you
want to learn about that, go read an academic book and
good luck at staying awake. This book is about the reality
of leadership.

Yes, I work with chief executives, and I also work with
information technology 'leaders', with community
'leaders', with The Children's Society and in many walks
of life.

I believe that the reality of leadership is very different
now from what it was, and from what it will be, very very
soon. It used to be about leaders and followers.

It is now about leaders being everyone and everywhere,
and to some degree always will.

A new wave of leadership is coming. Born out of the
belief that the future must be very different from the past,
this new wave of leadership says that leadership is about
discovering who we are, it is about living with integrity
and with values, and it is about playing our part on this
earth.

This book is about all three, however it is particularly about leadership now, and leadership arriving very soon, both of which have one common theme:

- **Everyone is a leader, that's every single person, including you; whether you choose to accept this leadership is your choice.**

And it is this new era of leadership, of personal identity and liberation, that forms the seventh principle of Naked Leadership.

The biggest mystery of life is to discover who we truly are. For when we discover this, no one can ever take this away from us.

The **seventh principle** says that the moment we were born, we were in a state of unlimited potential, inner bliss and perfect happiness, and that most of us then spend the rest of our lives seeking to feel the same, once again, before we die. Sadly few achieve this, but you can, if you so choose.

This book is about these seven principles, and how to harness, build and then release the awesome, unique powers that are already within you, right now. It is about self-discovery, it is about team/family/community/ organisational achievement, and it is about you and every-one else.

But it is about so much more than that. The biggest debate we had about *The Naked Leader* was, 'where does this book sit?' Is it a business book, a mind, body and spirit book, or a leadership of life book?

All three. This is a book about a new form of leadership;

it is based on the values of contribution, integrity and enlightenment, embedded in action and results.

The seven principles of Naked Leadership

1. Success is a formula, and it is simple.

2. This formula does not 'belong' to anyone – it belongs to everyone.

3. To be successful, you need rely on no one other than yourself.

4. Success is whatever you want it to be, it is yours to define.

5. Success can happen very fast, often in a heartbeat.

6. Everyone has value, can be anything they want, and is a leader.

7. The biggest mystery of life, is to discover who we truly are.

By the way, you do not need to know these seven principles for any of this book to 'work' (i.e. make a difference) for you. That would place this book amongst most other leadership books . . . 'oh, you didn't achieve that, well, you didn't learn principle three of Naked Leadership, go to jail, go directly to jail . . .'. I offer these principles as an introduction to the thinking, the style and the actions you will meet on your paths and adventure. They can be summarised as follows:

Naked Leadership – Giving people back to themselves

- **The gift of choice**: your future – your choice. Strip away the jargon of success, and with it the fear of failure. Define and personalise your success and your purpose, follow the guaranteed formula, take persistent action and be whatever you want to be. Success can happen in a single heartbeat, and when it happens for you, enjoy it. Do not compare yourself to others, or judge them, for they are on a different path, and as you do, live with passion, and with...

- **The clarity of values**: be true to yourself, every moment of every day. Reveal the answer to the greatest mystery of your life, who you truly are. Discover this and no one will ever be able to take it away from you. Be proud, and live with contribution, integrity and enlightenment. Everyone has value, so live for each other. Respect everyone, while celebrating differences. Help others less fortunate than you to find their path. Be at peace with yourself, the world and everyone in it, and you will experience . . .

- **The power of liberation**: you are an amazing, unique and special person. Everything you need to be anything you want is within you, waiting to be ignited. You need no reliance on others, for what lies before you, and what lies behind you, are but blades of grass to what lies within you. Look within, rediscover the unlimited potential of your first few moments on this earth, soar high, soar fast, and soar free.

Naked Leadership delivers

- **Powerful success**: Stripping away the mystery, hype and jargon, to share the single formula for guaranteed success, which is available to everyone, including you, right now.

- **Precise actions**: Revealing the exact, proven strategies and actions that will create immediate and lasting change, and transformation. What to do, when to do it, and exactly how to do it.

- **Profitable results**: Liberating your number one assets – you and your people. Inspiring deeply held belief and confidence, while releasing their awesome potential. It is powerful, and the results are amazing.

Before you begin your journey of leadership, and discovery (or you may be reading this book backwards, in which case this will be the last section you are reading!), let us once again revisit the formula for guaranteed success:

1. **Know where you want to go.**

2. **Know where you are now.**

3. **Know what you have to do, to get to where you want to go.**

4. **Do it!**

This book comprises 51 different inspirations. It doesn't matter what they are called – inspirational islands, chapters, columns, actions or wallpaper. The key point is that each and every one of them follows this four-stage approach.

1. **Where you will be after reading, and putting into action, this inspiration.**

2. **As you read, you will know your starting point, be honest about that.**

3. **You will select the key actions; what must be done.**

4. **You will know exactly how to do it.**

The room went completely silent for at least ten seconds. Over 400 people sitting, completely still. It was one of those professionally embarrassing, un-British moments, and no one knew what would happen next, least of all me.

I had just completed a presentation on cultural transformation, in my usual direct style, offering over 100 different ideas and actions that might help leaders to address the critically important areas of leadership, motivation and culture. I sat down – exhausted as I always am after presenting – and the chairman asked for the first question. A hand went up towards the back of the room.

'David, thank you for sharing your ideas with us today.'

I relaxed, this was going to be one of those friendly, warm, supportive questions. The hand continued,

'However, I have to say that I did not agree with anything you have said today, David, or with any of the actions you have suggested that we take.'

I was gobsmacked. Not because he disagreed with me, that often happens – and I love it when it does, not because he challenged me in front of so many people, again that happens many times. No, my reaction was that here was someone who disagreed with not just some of my ideas, but every single one!

'What do I say now?' I thought, 'how can I reply and avoid a negative, public confrontation with someone I have never even met before?'

I played for time.

'Tell me, are you happy, no, delighted, with everything in your company, (I almost added "life") and with how you and your team are treated, by your colleagues?'

'Of course not', he relied, 'but none of what you have suggested will help.' He seemed to be enjoying himself now, gathering momentum. There were several chuckles of laughter beginning to break out.

My career was finished, never would I speak anywhere again. I would retire to Hull.

And then it came to me.

'In that case,' I began, 'do the opposite.'

'Pardon?' he replied.

'Take everything I have said here today, and do the complete opposite', I said. I was beginning to warm to this man now, as he had helped me express something that I had long believed, but never articulated.

This was beginning to confuse him, which was not my intention at all, so I explained what I meant, which was basically this: If you are not content with something in your career, as a leader or in your life, do something about it. And if that action does not work, then do something else, and keep taking action until you achieve the result you desire. Whether it's staff morale, relationships, love, or the money you earn, talking, moaning and feeling bad counts for absolutely nothing. Consistent, focused and relentless action is everything.

This was the moment that Naked Leadership was born. It was the breakthrough in my thinking, and helped to explain why some ideas work spectacularly well in one organisation, but achieve nothing in another. Every single person, team and company is different, because as people we are all different – ideas, initiatives and theories are worthless if they do not lead to action.

And, with that action:

If you do what you have always done, you will get what you have always got.

And so, if you want a different outcome, you must do different things.

This may seem obvious to you, but it is one of the most powerful phrases in success. Look inside you and be honest, look around you and observe.

A quick example – your teenager has come home from school, and over tea you ask: 'What did you do at school today?' They reply: 'Nothing'.

Pause – this is the moment in which you can do something different, and achieve a different result, or do what you have always done, which is to repeat the same question, but this time, say it LOUDER (because clearly your son or daughter has a hearing defect) . . . To which they reply, 'NOTHING'. To which you say 'don't shout at me' (and the downward spiral begins). (Longer pause.)

Then you ask the same question again, but this time you say it both LOUDER and S-L-O-W-E-R, (because obviously your daughter or son has both a hearing defect and some learning difficulties). To which they reply, 'I T-O-L-D Y-O-U, N-O-T-H-I-N-G' and storm out of the room up to their bedroom. (Pause.) Then the spiral ends with you proclaiming: 'Kids today, they don't know how lucky they've got it' or similar.

Doing the same thing, over and over again, in our personal lives, at work or in anything that we do, and expecting a different result is pretty much the definition of madness. And yet, that's what we have done . . . until now, perhaps.

Here's a second key phrase:

There is no right or wrong, there is only what takes you closer to your dream, and what does not.

In this context I do not mean 'right' in a moral or ethical sense, I mean that we are bombarded with instructions, advice and offerings in how to move forward in our lives. Much of what we are told is conflicting, indeed, most leading 'experts' in being all that we can be disagree with each other, sometimes they are poles apart.

What I am suggesting is that none of these is right or wrong with what they offer. I am not right or wrong with what I offer in this book. This book will provide you with literally hundreds of real, specific and practical actions to take. Either take those that will help you get to where you want to go, and make them happen, or do the complete opposite. It is your choice.

You are now embarking on your journey, on one of seven paths of leadership. And you can switch journeys at any time you wish . . .

If you wish to go on Leadership of:

living as a leader

You have come from either:

47 'The Most Powerful Questions on Earth . . . Plus . . .'
(Leadership of Self)
or

32 'Values-based Leadership' (Leadership of Culture)
You are on Leadership of Self – 6 of 7

Most of the truly outstanding leaders in history, business, and life, have the common trait of a positive, certain, compelling belief system.

This is far deeper than positive thinking, and is at the very heart of personal, team and company achievement. We can apply the very best of belief systems to make this happen, fast.

Our subconscious mind is programmed to answer the questions we ask it. If we suffer delays on a business project and ask ourselves, 'Why does every project I work on always fail?' our subconscious mind will seek out all of the evidence to support this. It will immediately fill our mind, body and very being with scores of negative evidence to support this belief. If, on the other hand, we ask ourselves a more empowering question such as, 'How does this event help us to move forward, to achieve our goal?' we will receive a more helpful and positive response.

A few years ago I was asked to 'turnaround' a team providing frontline customer support. It was not in good shape, had no leadership or direction, its image in the company was very poor, and staff morale was rock bottom.

On the first day of my arrival, never having met any of the people, I gathered the team together and made a promise. If they believed in me, and each other, demonstrated loyalty and respect, and worked hard, we would achieve amazing things together.

I had no evidence that we could do this, in fact I had plenty of evidence that we could not. However I knew that the only way to turn events around was through the efforts and energies of these people before me, and the first stage of this was for them to believe we could do it. After just fifteen minutes of speaking, and sharing a more compelling future than they had ever heard, over a third of the department was with me. To paint a compelling picture, to inspire people onto a common journey, to ignite people's hearts and minds, we do not need to have detail, we need to know where we are going, and to believe in that journey.

The next six months were an effort, but never a struggle, and together, we transformed the department. People wanted to come to work, they put others before themselves, and they gave their best – each and every day. Personally I did very little, other than enabling others to be all that they could be, and having a solid, unshakeable, compelling belief in what we were doing. A single key to this was attaching powerful and enabling beliefs to each and every event, and realising that no event had any meaning other than the meaning we chose to give it.

Our belief systems determine how we see the world. We can believe whatever we choose, and we can alter our belief systems immediately. It's not what happens to us that counts, it's what we do about it.

Beliefs often make events self-fulfilling. You know the story – you have decided in your mind that you are not going to like something, or that you will get on well with someone when you meet them. From then, you are looking out for every piece of evidence to support this belief. Guess what? What you believed will happen, happens. Then of course you say, 'See – I told you so'.

As leaders, we must choose our beliefs with great care, because our beliefs will determine our future, and that of our people and organisation.

George B. Dantiz was a student at the University of California in Berkeley. Arriving late to a statistics class he copied the problems he saw on the board, thinking that they were homework, and handed in his solutions several days later. The two problems were not a homework assignment; they were problems previously thought to be unsolvable which the instructor had used as examples in his lecture that day.

(The story also sets the plot in motion in the recent movie Good Will Hunting.)
and . . .

Throughout our lives we will all be tested and challenged in a variety of different ways. W Mitchell was certainly tested. He endured tremendous pain and insurmountable obstacles almost beyond belief. Despite the never-ending pain he went through, he hung in there with his unwavering determination and indefatigable will power. At age 28, living a wonderful life, he had a motorcycle accident.

Over 65% of his body was severely burned. The leather motorcycle jacket saved most of his body, but didn't save his hands. His helmet saved his life, but did little to save his face. While he was in a coma for two weeks, the doctors hid the one thing they feared would kill him once he woke up – and that was a mirror. They feared the shock of seeing himself after the accident with his badly burned, distorted new face just might be too much for him. The doctors were wrong; unbelievably, he endured the process.

From that incident, Mitchell became passionate to share his story that you could look like a monster on the outside and still be a good person – warm, funny, and caring – on the inside.

'Before I was paralysed, there were 10,000 things that I could do. Now there are 9000. I can either dwell on the 1000 I lost, or focus on the 9000 I have left,' Mitchell states bravely.

Just when everything seemed to be smooth sailing again, the unbelievable happened. Back doing the hobby he loved – flying – Mitchell's plane crashed when the wings iced up on takeoff. 'It appears you will never walk again.

It appears you'll have to use a wheelchair for the rest of your life,' whispered his doctor.

'Why me? I laid in bed and wondered if there was anything left of my life,' reflects Mitchell. There certainly was, despite what had happened. In the hospital, he met a pretty, young nurse who assisted him, named Annie Baker. A few years later, to everyone's amazement but Mitchell's, he married her.

Today, Mitchell is one of the world's top motivational public speakers giving over 70 talks per year to audiences around the world. He has also been awarded the prestigious CPAE, Council of Peers Award of Excellence – the highest award for professionalism bestowed by the National Speakers Association.

If you wish to stay on Leadership of Self, go to **Synchronicity**, 8 (p71)
or
If you wish to change journey, join **Leadership of Teams**, go to **Project Success**, 28 (p177)

our secret driving forces

You have come from either:

1   'The Structure of Guaranteed Success'
or
19   'Room 101' (Leadership of Culture)
You are on Leadership of People – 1 of 7

People buy from people. People motivate, promote and sack people and, although our future is in our own hands, we need others to help us achieve it. How we interact with other human beings is critical to personal, team and organisational success.

Much can be learned, and achieved, from exploring people's *similarities*, what we all have in common.

Research differs on the precise wording of these, and on their exact positioning, but the vast majority of researchers agree on the top five human motivators that apply to us all.

This information is hardly 'inside-knowledge' – being almost universally agreed by psychologists over many years, however, they are secret in the sense that few people talk about them!

1 A sense of personal power and mastery over others

The strongest driver for human beings. Many people will not admit it in public, or even acknowledge it in private. Think about gossip, job titles, or how you feel when you hear that a business rival is not doing as well as you.

Like it or not, it plays a major part in all of us.

2 A sense of personal pride, and importance

This is a feeling within ourselves, of something we stand for. Some may call it ego, or personal status. If you do not believe the importance of this one, try changing some-one's job title to 'administration assistant', or introduce the word 'consultant' into your organisation!

3 Financial security and success

Money remains one of the strongest personal drivers and material wealth one of the most powerful displays of how we are doing.

4 Reassurance of self-worth and recognition of efforts

We all strive to be reassured that what we are doing is OK, we often seek out and value the opinions of others over those of ourselves. This covers everything from the power of a well-timed 'thank-you' to promotion issues etc.

5 Peer approval and acceptance

People identify with specific groups – with other business leaders, in a club or in a social setting. We all crave to be accepted by people we identify with.

This list is controversial. Whenever people are asked in public what drives them, more often than not they will give the politically correct answer of 'caring for others' or 'accomplishment of something worthwhile'. Although high in the list of human motivators, not in the top five.

Whatever you think of this list, or will admit to with regard to your personal goals and drivers, they hold strong messages that we can apply in all of our communications.

However it is amazing how few businesses and management fads take them into account, in any form. As leadership, motivation and human potential become absolutely crucial to personal and business achievement, this list should be borne in mind when we are involved in any, and all, human interactions.

Remember, always, there is no right or wrong, there is only what serves you, and what does not.

A man is at Heathrow airport with an important client. He sees Bill Gates sitting in the corner. When his client goes for a walk he approaches Bill to ask him a favour.

'Bill, really sorry to disturb you, my name is Mike, and I

wonder if you would do me a favour. I am with a very important customer. Would you mind terribly coming over in a few minutes, and just say Hi, to make it look like we know each other.'

Bill agrees, and sure enough, when he sees the client has returned, he wanders over towards them, he taps Mike on the shoulder:

'Hi Mike, great to see you again.'

To which Mike replies:

'Oh, get lost Bill, can't you see I'm busy?'

If you wish to stay on Leadership of People, go to **Leadership in Times of War** 49 (p313)
or
If you wish to change journey, join **Leadership of Self**, go to **Jargon Free NLP!** 22 (p141)

a leader's biggest timewasters

You have come from either:

51 'Leadership by E-Mail' (Leadership of Company)
or

24 'Skills of Leadership over Management' (Leadership of Skills)
You are on Leadership of Company – 6 of 7

Business leaders carry out many time consuming activities that yield little value.

They are, in reverse order of wasted time:

⑤ Budgeting: The annual budget round has at times

descended into farce, in particular:

- guessing the cost and benefit of projects;
- hiding the cost of training inside other cost codes, as it is the first target for cutback; and
- ensuring that as end of year approaches the budget is spent in full, for fear that coming in under budget will lead to it being reduced the following year:

Tip: Be clear on what you want to achieve first, then budget, not the other way around.

4 **Accessing the right information, at the right time**: Excessive Information Systems have a lot to answer for. Often, they have done little more than produce more paper and irrelevant detail. As a result, ad hoc reports continue to be hard-coded, and some companies rely more on self-developed spreadsheets.

Tip: be clear what you need to know to drive your company forward, and focus on that.

3 **Playing e-mail tag, or the cc game**: Far from making life easier and more effective, e-mails have over-complicated the communications process, and many people now write e-mails when none are needed. Furthermore, there seems to be little evidence of e-mail etiquette, with most hassles and wasted time being caused by aggressive/inaccurate mails. This is made ten times worse by other people being copied on the e-mail, often to make a point, sometimes to simply drop the recipient in it.

Tip: Don't start the cc game, and make all e-mails positive, no matter what the provocation. Count to 100 before replying to a provocative e-mail (if you are really busy ask someone to count for you).

② **Finding out who owns what**: Damning indeed. Who owns what in the complex world of today's medium and large companies seems to be a growing concern. When things go wrong inside their company, ownership becomes someone else's hot potato. As a leader you need to know who is accountable, for praise as well as other actions.

Tip: For mission-critical projects, publish accountability. Naked Leaders take public ownership for everything that goes wrong, no matter what, and praise for nothing. Praise always belongs to other people, and is most powerful when it is specific.

① **Attendance at internal meetings**: The runaway winner. Few of these seem to follow any formal structure or reach clear action-based decisions and results; most are an excuse for politics.

Tip: Set a clear, defined outcome at the start of the meeting – and review if it has been achieved.

This list has less to do with time management than sanity preservation. They may all have a part to play in our lives, but we can equally play a part by taking control of each, and the many other low value tasks not included here.

Open Forums are not time wasters, they are time investors. One of the most direct, immediate and powerful ways to demonstrate openness, find out what is happening around you, and meet your people. A few years ago a leader I know started them in his department. It was staggering – over half of his team turned up at the first, and they became a regular event.

They carried on for several months, and then the numbers attending started to fall. At one point he was literally on his own. So he decided to cancel them. He wrote an e-mail to his department and said they had been stopped, owing to lack of interest. This was a mistake, and all of his other cultural work fell apart.

The fewer people who attend your open forums, the better, but you must still provide them, even if no one else comes along (the ultimate compliment to you as an open leader). It's a bit like party invitations, people want to be invited, but they may choose not to come along.

If you wish to stay on Leadership of Company, go to **Oh, I've Had Such a Curious Dream!** 25 (p161)

or

If you wish to change journey, join **Leadership of Culture, go to Following the Lines and Breaking the Rules** 21 (p135)

the power of mentoring

5

You have come from either:

50 'The 7 Greatest Conspiracies of Success'
(Leadership of Career)
or
'Your Personality Becomes Their Personality . . .'
27 (Leadership of Teams)
You are on Leadership of Career – 2 of 7

How much time do we have to help others along the way? In our busy lives, what value do we place on the time spent enabling others to perform better, and to be all that they can be? What are the consequences if we do not? High staff turnover and recruitment costs, low effectiveness and the inability to capture the ideas, experience and talent that lie dormant within our own people.

Many companies, and leaders, have turned to mentoring. It is a hugely powerful skill.

What is mentoring?

Mentoring is when one person (the mentor) helps another (the mentee) to transform their knowledge, work or overall thinking. This happens in one-to-one meetings, at which the mentor invites the mentee to talk, and the mentor asks relevant, searching, non-threatening questions to allow the mentee to discover the 'answers' for themselves.

What are the qualities of a mentor?

1. A mentor is someone who is, above everything else, totally trustworthy.

2. A mentor must be patient – real long-term learning can take time. However they must also be persistent in ensuring that mentoring sessions stay on track.

3. A mentor's status is irrelevant; it is the interpersonal qualities that count.

4. A mentor must be able to ask the right questions to address deep-rooted issues.

5. Someone who is committed to making the relationship work on all levels.

The benefits of a mentor – to the person being mentored

- A mentor can assist, and transform, personal and career development.
- He or she can also be a sounding board, perhaps before a major presentation.
- If the mentor is more senior, there are opportunities to learn. Perhaps you can learn from a leader in your organisation.
- With a mentor, people feel the organisation is taking a genuine interest in them, and what they are trying to achieve. This is highly motivating.

The benefits of a mentor – to the person doing the mentoring

- Self-discovery through helping others.
- Learning about areas of the department they would not otherwise know about.
- Sense of achievement when mentee achieves, and meets objectives.
- Fostering closer relationships, communication and trust at all levels.

The experience, ideas and contributions people can make must be brought out in the most positive, constructive and motivational way. Mentoring is the most effective, powerful and long-lasting method of achieving this.

René Carayol, bestselling author of Corporate Voodoo, *on mentoring:*

1 Identify your own Personal Sorcerer.

There is no better feeling than knowing you have your own personal trainer or mentor. Being the Sorcerer's Apprentice can be massively rewarding, if the Sorcerer is a person of great wisdom and standing in your eyes.

There are three steps in the process.

Step One: Identify the traits you would really like to have. Establish how you would like to be seen and remembered.

STOP NOW! WRITE THEM DOWN HERE.

THE CHARACTERISTICS, QUALITIES, VALUES AND BEHAVIOURS THAT I WOULD MOST LIKE TO LIVE BY ARE:

HEALTH WARNING: IF YOU CAN'T WRITE THEM DOWN, THEN YOU'RE LIVING IN SOMEONE ELSE'S VOODOO

Step Two: Now identify which person that you know of demonstrates that behaviour as a matter of course. Hopefully, this will be someone that you know or know of, and perhaps a friend of a friend, or a colleague of an acquaintance.

STOP NOW! WRITE THEM DOWN HERE

The quality	The Sorcerer for this quality
1	
2	
3	
4	
5	

Step Three: Now approach these people. Ask them if they will be your mentor (your Sorcerer). It may sound impossible to achieve, or an imposition to ask of someone: but remember we all have egos, and most people will be flattered even to be approached in this way. Most Sorcerers will want to have their spells live on.

Nelson Mandela said recently in London that 'unsolicited advice is rarely listened to or respected. But solicited advice is treated with due care and attention, and creates bonds that are rarely broken or forgotten.' Great Sorcerers can share many years of learning, wisdom and experience in a very short space of time, if the apprentice has the ability to listen, hear and act on the ingredients and recipes that are being shared.

Voodoo is rarely written learning, it is handed down from generation to generation, sometimes through great war stories, feats of derring-do, fables and some great contemporary urban myths. Sorcerers paint vivid pictures that are easily kept in one's mind's eye. Bob Marley called this his 'Natural Mystic'. It is this Natural Mystic that does not fit with conformance cultures, but is the oxygen of your personal Voodoo.

Know why you've chosen them

The choice of Sorcerer needs to be taken seriously, and you must aim as high as you can. Ideally, your prospective Sorcerer should know you or of you, but this is not essential. They must be someone that you inherently respect and look up to. Their position and knowledge should be aspirational for you. There should be a significant gap between their experience and wisdom and your own.

Ask for what you want

You will feel that they are too busy or important to give up their precious time for you. Do not let this feeling put you off at all, rather think how wonderful it would be if they were your personal mentor. Once you have settled on a short list of three or four people make contact immediately – there is no reason to wait. It is helpful to go through a common acquaintance to broker a meeting, but this is not essential; just make contact.

Make it easy for them

All you are asking for is an hour or two every couple of months. Offer to perform all the necessary legwork to make the meetings happen; organise all the meetings, preferably in their office (to make it easy for them), prepare any agenda or discussion points in advance. It is important to stress the confidential nature of these relationships, and that nothing said in the meeting would be mentioned outside. This is imperative to enable the mentor to feel at ease. Offer to try one and see how it goes for both parties. The only measure of success is that the two parties want to keep on meeting. It will just die if either party is not benefiting from the relationship. Remember, Sorcerers can pick up a trick or two from their apprentices, sometimes just the confidence and pride the relationship can give off is return enough. The real drug for the Sorcerer is to be involved in the growth of precocious talent.

If at first you don't succeed, be all the more determined next time around. The benefit of being a mentee is seriously worth a couple of rejections to get there.

If you wish to stay on Leadership of Career, go to **Integrity-based Networking** 17 (p115)
or
If you wish to change journey, join **Leadership of People,** go to **Our Next Generation** 40 (p253)

job evaluation in the bin

You have come from either:

18 'Organisational De-structures' (Leadership of Company)

or

46 'The Five Pitfalls of Leadership' (Leadership of Career)

You are on Leadership of Company – 3 of 7

I will never forget the day I got the call. I had been 'selected' to serve for one year on the Job Evaluation Panel. In the opinion of the HR Director, one of the most important, prestigious, exciting experiences of corporate life.

The 'panel' was shrouded in such secrecy that it made MI5 look like Max Clifford. All of the documents, 'evidence' and tomes that arrived before the meeting were marked – strictly confidential, for addressees only. The biggest batch, so thick you could use it to access your loft at home, came with a supporting note saying: 'not to be sent by e-mail'!!!

After one reading I could see why no one outside the panel should be allowed to read the documentation – it was so excruciatingly, mind-numbingly boring that it would have instantly driven them to suicide. However, for me it had one great side effect. Having been instructed to 'file at home', I did so, next to my bed. Forget relaxing music or get-to-sleep tapes, this stuff worked every time. I have never slept so well.

The day of my first panel meeting arrived, I left for the off-site meeting armed with my two trees worth of paper, and entered probably the single worst day of my working life, ever. It started with my being welcomed to the panel, and being told it might take a while for me to 'know the ropes'. I wish there had been a few ropes around, I could have made it out through the roof.

Eight hours of total, utter, absolute boredom, garbage and irrelevance, only punctuated by my calculations that each meeting was costing the company over £5000 in lost time and salaries.

I resigned from the panel the very next day.

Aside from the procedural issues, which many organisations still adopt, and which are usually farcical in the extreme, there is a serious underlying issue in job evaluation, job descriptions and this ongoing focus on roles and not people.

A few years ago, these systems were introduced for

various reasons:

- jobs and titles could be clearly defined, and broken down;
- organisations were easily broken down into clear departments; and
- structure and stability were the order of the day.

Naked Leaders know that job descriptions and related activities have no role, requirement or relevance because:

- roles are changing every day – flexibility is king;
- organisational structures are now unclear;
- people are more important than jobs; and
- speed is crucial.

And so, what should organisations do to save time, trees, hassle, money and focus on the important?

1. **Replace job descriptions with people descriptions – in effect, structured CVs.**

2. **Ensure people are encouraged to learn new skills and to work across any area of an organisation.**

3. **Reward people through 360-degree appraisals (by your boss, peers, self and team) and self-determined salary increases, in which teams decide how much they should receive individually.**

What I am proposing may sound extreme – it is not. What is extreme is the way so many age-old, tired and pointless procedures and rules have survived for so long. One thing is for sure, the longer they survive, the shorter their companies will.

A man in a hot air balloon realised he was lost. He reduced altitude and spotted a woman below. He descended a bit more and shouted: 'Excuse me, can you help me? I promised a friend I would meet him an hour ago but I don't know where I am.'

The woman below replied: 'You are in a hot air balloon hovering approximately 30 feet above the ground. You are between 40 and 41 degrees north latitude and between 59 and 60 degrees west longitude.'

'You must be an engineer', said the balloonist.

'I am', replied the woman, 'How did you know?'

'Well', answered the balloonist, 'everything you told me is technically correct, but I still have no idea what to make of your information, and the fact is I am still lost. Frankly, you've not been much help so far.'

The woman below responded, 'You must be in management.'

'I am', replied the balloonist, 'but how did you know?'

'Well', said the woman, 'you don't know where you are or where you are going. You have risen to where you are, due to a large quantity of hot air. You made a promise which you have no idea how to keep, and you expect people beneath you to solve your problems. The fact is you are in exactly the same position you were in before we met, but now, somehow, it's my fault.'

(With thanks to Philip Allen)

If you wish to stay on Leadership of Company, go to
Hidden Account Management 34 (p221)
or
If you wish to change journey join **Leadership of Self**, go
to **The Power of State – Everyone Needs a Place to Be**
29 (p183)

reverse headhunting –
get your own back

You have come from either:

10 'Leaders Are Born and Not Made!' (Leadership of People)

or

15 'Your Team – From Good to Unstoppable' (Leadership of Teams)

You are on Leadership of People – 6 of 7

Resignation from a company is fraught with different emotions. Behind the statistics (it costs three times more to replace someone than to train them), beyond the procedures (please complete this form indicating lost skills), and beneath all of the surface professionalism (we are not surprised) lie the real feelings. The feeling of the first call from the headhunter, of finding the 'ideal' position, the joy so often felt as one resigns, and the secret panic in the organisation as you do so. Then, after you have left, the discovery that the grass may not always be greener, the inevitable contractor taken on to fill the gap (they will stay forever) and the blame – you are suddenly the reason that everything has gone wrong.

Quite apart from reducing the cost of losing people, the talents they take with them, and the time to replace them, there must be a better way of doing things.

There is; reverse headhunting. It involves staying in direct contact with those people who leave your organisation, whose skills, personality or presence you will sorely miss, with a view to them returning to your organisation at some stage.

When someone decides to leave a company, it usually happens like this. They are first attracted by a particular position, either through seeing an advert or receiving a call from a headhunter. Regardless of their success with that position, the moment this happens for them, their mind has switched into thinking about leaving their present employer.

When this happens it is often just a matter of time before a person will leave, as with this new mindset they will be actively looking for something new.

How can Naked Leaders encourage people to see their present company as appealing as any other, and if you do lose a key person, how can you get them back again?

Firstly, we can ensure that people see and treat their present position on equal terms to any they may apply for.

How do we do this?

- **Write out compelling descriptions for the positions you have, as if it were a recruitment campaign – make sure they are available for all.**
- **Keep people's CVs and skills up to date for them**

Secondly, reverse headhunt. Do this by keeping in close contact with anyone who leaves, whom you really need. I am not recommending that you stalk them, merely that you call them now and again to see how they are, and to let them know they would always be welcome back in your company. Let them know of the cultural improvements you are making. Also, ensure that people who leave your organisation are not blamed for anything – this is not easy, but when you set the trend for this, others will follow.

One word of warning – don't bring people back in more senior roles; if you do, word will spread like wildfire that the best way to be promoted is to resign!

Remember, you are not reverse headhunting the person back into the position they left; that will have been filled by now. You are bringing them back because of who they are and the value they add to your organisation.

Reverse headhunting is now used by several organisations with stunning results, cost savings and, most importantly, reignited talent and potential.

Reverse headhunting gives us an excellent start on where to look when we need to recruit new people . . .

The Mullah Nasrudin was outside his house under a lamp-post one evening scrabbling on the pavement.

'What are you looking for?' said one of his neighbours.

'I've lost my key', he said. The neighbour knelt down to help him look, and as they searched some more passers-by began to help as well – but they could not find the key.

'Are you sure you dropped the key out here?' said the neighbour.

'Oh no', said Nasrudin, 'I dropped it in the garden.'

'So why are we searching here?'

'There's no light in the garden.'

If you wish to stay on Leadership of People, go to **Doom or Disaster, Welcome to Neg-Land** 20 (p129)

or

If you wish to change journey, join **Leadership of Career**, go to **Your CV Stands, or Falls, For You** 13 (p93)

synchronicity

You have come from either:

2   'Living as a Leader' (Leadership of Self)
or

35   'Making Success so Easy, and Failure Impossible to Achieve' (Leadership of Teams)
You are on Leadership of Self – 7 of 7

In all of my leadership work, there is no doubt what captures people's imagination more than anything else – synchronicity, or meaningful coincidences.

Coincidence implies that two events have happened at the same time, as if by chance. However, it is possible to define two different types of coincidence. The first involves pure chance where there seems to be no particular significance in the coincidental events. The second type of coincidence is when the event seems to be full of significance.

Carl Jung labelled such events as 'synchronicity'. The type of event may seem to the outside world to be meaningless chance, but to the person who experiences it, the opposite is true and the event is full of meaning.

In leadership and personal development circles, it has become a hot topic, driven largely by the success of James Redfield's publishing phenomenon, *The Celestine Prophecy*.

I believe in synchronicity at three levels. On a basic level, it happens to all of us, and we need to look out for it happening. This level is a reflection that all of our lives are interconnected in some way, and our reaction to these events is usually one of amazement, disbelief, and feeling good. These events happen all around us, every day.

We move to the next level when we widen our vision and take in more of life around us. I am often told this happens when someone becomes pregnant; suddenly all they see around them are pregnant women, babies and magazines about childbirth! And so it is with our beliefs, the way we see the world. When we believe something to be true we see the world in that way. (A classic example of that is when we ask our son or husband – sorry it has to be male! – to bring in the salt, or something from the fridge, or whatever. They will stand right in front of the item and claim it is not there. That is because they have convinced themselves they will not find it, and so they do not.)

This level is linked to the strength of our beliefs, convictions and certainty. I firmly believe that life stands

THE NAKED LEADER

aside for those who know where they are going, and when we as individuals, teams or companies are absolutely clear, focused and certain of what we are going to achieve, events will conspire to help us.

This will happen automatically, for two reasons. Firstly because success really does breed success – when a project team is together, as one, and driving forward they will remove barriers, leap hurdles and attract the resources they need. Secondly, because when we know where we are going, we will always be looking out for events, people and support to help us get there. Isn't it strange that, in our culture, we are more than happy to believe in negative 'self-fulfilling prophecies', while being less inclined to accept the positive parallels?

The deepest level of synchronicity is when we simply expect such events to happen as part of our everyday lives. This is the most challenging to accept. However, people who talk about experiencing this third level can provide scores of examples that happen to them every single day. And yet those who do not believe in it experience none, on any day. Now there's a clue.

A clear, compelling vision, combined with total belief in its achievement, and action, will be enough to open your eyes to the synchronicity that is already happening around you, in your career, project and personal life.

It is interesting to look across many departments, companies and business in general. Without exception those with a clear vision, and positive certainty, almost always succeed, and those who see life as a roulette wheel, or each day as a disaster, almost always fail. Whether that is evidence depends on what you believe, of course.

Synchronicity gives us a sense of hope, a sense that some-

thing bigger is happening out there than what we can see, which is especially important in times like this when there are so many reasons for despair.

If your belief system is such that intuition and synchronicity are real and significant, you will notice them.

If your belief system is that they're hogwash, you won't.

Carolyn North *Synchronicity: The Anatomy of Coincidence*

I could fill this book with synchronicities from me and others, I select just three that are pretty amazing.

Paul Downs

'I had offered to secure an entertaining and enlightening speaker for our school AGM of which I am governor. I had in mind a gentleman called Dr Chris Yapp who I had met once before. I wasn't sure how I was going to approach him but I felt confident I would find a way. The very next day I was called by a colleague inviting me to attend a summer dinner in the City of London, at which she was hosting a table. Who was I sitting next to at the dinner? Chris Yapp! I spoke to him about my school and whether he would consider providing the keynote speech, he agreed that he would do it if his diary permitted.'

Claire Reid

'When trying to find a school of which to be a governor, I had made numerous enquiries and phone calls to the relevant bodies to try and find a school that required a governor. After several months of writing and leaving lots of phone calls I was about to give up and channel my energies into something else. Then out of the blue came a letter asking me if I would like to be a school governor for my local school round the corner from where I lived. I agreed willingly. After some investigation I discovered that this invitation was completely random and was in no way connected to my original enquiries!'

And just one from me . . .

A friend told me about a new book, Conversations With God, which was taking the US by storm. I decided to buy it the next day. However, when I got home a book was waiting for me in the post. Having ordered a sports book online a few days before, I opened the envelope looking forward to brushing up on my squash. But they made a mistake and sent the wrong book, guess which book I received...

What about you?

Was there someone who you met 'by accident' on the train? Or an article you happened to see that related to something in your life? Think about what it may mean for you. It only becomes synchronicity if you act on the event. What will happen to you today, who will you meet, that will have a huge influence on your life?

You have completed Leadership of Self, go to **Enlightened Leadership** 42 (p263)
or
If you wish to change journey, join **Leadership of Skills,** go to **Skills of Leadership over Management** 24 (p153)

who's to blame?

You have come from either:

11   'Balance The Sources Of Power'
(Leadership of Culture)
or
'Building Total and Absolute Rapport'
41   (Leadership of Skills)
You are on Leadership of Culture – 5 of 7

Whodunnits seem to be very 'in' at the moment. *Midsomer Murders*, a revival of Agatha Christie novels, and a surge of interest inside organisations. I am not talking about the stabbings in the back that happen all the time, I am talking about something much more sinister . . .

who made all those decisions that went wrong?

It is no problem finding people who made the right decisions, you can find them in company magazines, on the notice board, or walking around the offices with a sticker on their backs saying 'I'm the clever one'. Indeed, sometimes there are far more people taking ownership, credit, and glory even, for things that go well, than there are people in an organisation! However, just try to find the person who took all the risky decisions that may have gone wrong, and you will draw a blank.

Take your organisation, for instance. Who exactly . . .

- **Owns that mission critical project that has been renamed 'suicide'?**
- **Sets the agenda for the future?**
- **Co-ordinates all those business initiatives?**
- **Calls in all those consultants?**
- **Writes such boring and irrelevant manuals?**
- **Invented performance related pay?**
- **Decided what acronyms we should use, to confuse our customers?**

I used to think that no one knows that, inside every organisation, decision making has grown so time consuming, complex and confusing that no one person will ever be held accountable for anything. But the number of people who have made excellent decisions all their lives scotched that one.

Then I was told it was the last person who left the department or company. However, this also failed to add up – how could a business analyst who left the company in 1998 be responsible for the latest project disaster, many years later? After years of exhaustive investigation, I can now reveal the answer. I now know who makes all the big decisions inside every organisation, indeed inside every department.

It is all very hush-hush, you understand, so please come closer to the page so that I can whisper it to you.

The answer is 'them'.

Think about it. Whenever you ask who took key global decisions that are not popular, or have gone wrong, the answer will be 'they did'.

And so, clearly, lying deep inside every organisation, we have 'them'. 'They' are directly responsible for each and every decision that can't be pinned on an individual.

Is it the board, the next level management group, your boss, or the others in your team?

You might think it is a bit dramatic to liken all this to the world of murder mystery, but that is exactly what is happening here. 'They' are being blamed for everything that goes wrong, and the associated grapevine, gossip and negativity is slowly strangling our companies and cultures.

So, my advice is that if you want a blameless, simple, nothing life then never ask questions, give an opinion, take ownership, take a risk, put your name to anything, talk to anyone, or even breathe too loudly, just in case.

On the other hand . . .

Do this. For a period of one week, resolve to say only positive things about everyone, especially behind their back to other people. OK, for one day if a week is too much. Do this, and see how great you feel. (This does not mean you do not tackle difficult issues, you will of course still do this, with the person concerned, in confidence.)

And a wonderful PS. Next team meeting go around the room and ask each person in turn to say what they most love about being in the team. Then ask each other person for one specific reason why it is great to have that person in the team. Make sure you allow enough time to cover everyone. No need to prepare – people give their best off the cuff.

As human beings one of the reasons we do not give praise is because often we are not very comfortable at accepting it. This has a double negative effect – we do not accept other people's genuine compliments, and they feel their positive comment has been thrown back in their face.

The best way to do this is to open an emotional bank account; you can do this right now and no one need ever know. Every time someone says something nice to you, look at them directly in the eyes, say a warm 'thank you' and mentally deposit in your bank account. See how you feel one week later. (One chap I know does this and makes a loud 'ding' noise as he makes each deposit. This may work for him, I would not recommend it as people may think you are barmy!)

If you wish to stay on Leadership of Culture, go to **Leadership by Magazine** 31 (p205)
or
If you wish to change journey, join **Leadership of Company,** go to **Leadership by E-Mail** 51 (p333)

leaders are born and not made!

You have come from either:

40 'Our Next Generation' (Leadership of People)
or

22 'Jargon Free NLPI (Leadership of Self)
You are on Leadership of People – 5 of 7

'Yes, there's one, and another . . .'

Many people believe that leaders are born, and not made. Presumably newborn leaders behave in a different way from other babies. It is almost worth a trip to the maternity hospital to check this out!

In reality, this belief is more often than not an excuse

used by some people to justify a lack of leadership behaviour in themselves. Of course we can all learn to be leaders, we can change our beliefs, our behaviours and our personalities. If we could not, our attitudes would be the same when we are 20, 40 and 60.

There are no 'born' leaders, however we are all born with unique strengths that help us in our leadership journeys – they are within us, and with most people they stay within. The notion that leaders are born, and others therefore will never be leaders, is illogical, depressing and seriously limiting to every human being. The idea suggests that the moment babies are born they either have the genetics to be a leader, or they do not. This argument would be fine if the definition of leadership and leaders had been constant for the past fifty years, but it is not. Indeed, more has been discovered about leadership and human behaviour in the last twenty years than in the previous thousand.

Furthermore, the 'born' argument does not take into account the effect that experience and learning has on our personalities, behaviours and on our inner selves.

Leadership is a skill and a habit. Like most skills and habits, one that improves with practice. As we become more skilled – the habit takes over – we worry less about the mechanics of doing it and focus more on the outcomes to be achieved.

And so it is with personality, much of personality is a set of responses that have become habits. Often these were developed with little forethought or awareness in school or at home. Presented with a challenge we respond, if it works we remember it and use it again. If it works often enough, we use it without too much thought and it becomes a habit. Take any set of habits, mix and stir, and we create our own unique approach to life.

But like any habit, we can choose to change. Much long-lasting negative behaviour can be altered.

Being human is wonderful. We can learn new ways, new skills, and ignore old habits. By taking the time to make better choices, new behaviours will become new habits.

One word of caution, many people will tell us that changing in this way is hard, requires struggle and is fraught with failure. We must be gentle with these people, reminding them that none of us are the same people we were last year and won't be the same this time next year.

My genuine belief and advice is this – every individual, team and organisation should strive to be all that they can be. To do this, you will have to be outstanding leaders and, provided you are ready for the challenge, you too can be all that you can be.

If you do believe leaders are born and cannot be made, then please, please believe you were born in the right part of the hospital . . . At a conference a few years ago someone took an extreme exception to my belief that leaders are made and not born. He was very aggressive in his questioning. I invited him to nominate any single person he knew, whom he did not think was born a leader, and I would spend one day with that person. In the conference he refused, but afterwards e-mailed me to say the person he would like to nominate was himself! We had a wonderful, cutting-edge and breakthrough day together. Breakthrough for both of us. He has asked not to be named, and he still believes leaders are born and not made. The difference is, he now believes he is one of the lucky ones!

If you wish to stay on Leadership of People, go to
Reverse Headhunting – Get Your Own Back 7 (p67)
or
If you wish to change journey, join **Leadership of Career,**
go to **The Five Pitfalls of Leadership** 46 (p293)

THE NAKED LEADER

balance the
sources of power

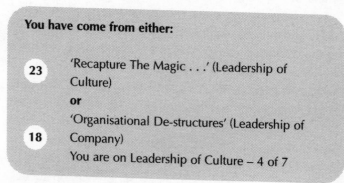

You have come from either:

23 'Recapture The Magic . . .' (Leadership of Culture)

or

18 'Organisational De-structures' (Leadership of Company)
You are on Leadership of Culture – 4 of 7

Everywhere we look, we see the words culture, balance and stress. Seemingly out of nowhere, business leaders are at last realising the importance of releasing the true potential, and total power, of their people.

Everywhere we listen, we hear people say there is more to life than work, indeed more to life than the one they are living.

Yet, despite the talk, and some positive examples, we continue to work harder than ever. In our organisations, we rush around in circles, on multiple projects with no real definition, and certainly no real benefit. We often look like no more than a bunch of well-meaning individuals stumbling through minefields in pursuit of an ill-defined goal, which keeps changing.

Just as we realise we need to slow down, we speed up. We design ever more complex solutions aimed at making our lives so much easier, but now having the reverse effect. It is their ease of use that lies at the heart of the cause. Every day we are bombarded with messages – e-mails, pagers and mobile phones – enabling people to be contacted not on the basis of where they may be, but where they actually are.

We always thought life was supposed to be for living, but for many it has become little more than an existence. So many people view work as a way of filling the hours between breakfast and dinner.

There is good news. A big difference today is that more people are aware, and determined to do something about it. The new century brings with it an opportunity to shape a new era of personal and business thinking, based on the simple premise that the future is not what it used to be.

It is a future based on simplicity of purpose, on success being measured not by material possessions, but by contribution, and on people discovering what they really want to do, and who they really are.

It is a way of life in which we take back control of our own lives, and in which:

THE NAKED LEADER

- companies realise the only way people will give their best, is if they want to;
- we recognise that there are more important things than physical possessions;
- we fulfil the demands of our work without being controlled by it;
- people are valued as free spirits, with ideas and imaginations unbounded; and
- humans truly become 'Beings' rather than 'Doings'.

Many leaders now talk openly about this new business age, some referring to it as the spiritual revolution. The 'Mind, Body and Spirit' sections of bookshops now outsell most others, and many of them cover themes just as applicable in the business world.

The great irony for those with a focus on finance is this – by releasing people's energy, by aligning individuals more closely with their organisations, and by improving the real quality of life for their staff, companies will be bound to improve their bottom line; it will be automatic.

Many thousands of people are realising there is more to life than their present realities, and that to reclaim their true selves does not mean having to 'drop out', indeed, quite the reverse. It means reaching new levels of energy, focus and contentment.

As with human beings, so with organisations, who are at last waking up to the fact that without their people they are nothing.

Somewhere deep beneath the layers of dust, fear and limiting beliefs that have attached themselves to our lives, is the feeling that there is more, so much more; that our lives to date have been but a blade of grass compared to what we can be. I urge you all to throw off those layers, and start to discover who you really are, no matter how well it may be hidden.

I was in Barcelona doing two presentations: 'Gaining real business benefits from IT systems', and 'How to overcome stress'. The first had 27 people, the second over 80. At the start I asked how many people in the room were suffering from stress, right now. No one put up their hands. I asked how many of them were attending because they knew someone who was suffering from stress, and they all put their hands up! I knew then that most of them were British!!

From The Balance – *The Moody Blues*
(lyrics by Graeme Edge)

Just open your eyes,
And realise, the way it's always been.
Just open your mind
And you will find
The way it's always been.
Just open your heart,
And that's a start.

If you wish to stay on Leadership of Culture, go to **Who's To Blame?** 9 (p77)
or
If you wish to change journey, join **Leadership of Skills**, go to **The Choice of Opposites** 44 (p279)

THE NAKED LEADER

charisma in a heartbeat!

You have come from either:

41 'Building Total and Absolute Rapport'
(Leadership of Skills)
or
'Your CV Stands, or Falls, for You' (Leadership of
13 Career)
You are on Leadership of Skills – 3 of 7

I was at a conference structured like *Question Time*. One
question from the audience of business leaders was on the
subject of charisma. A chief executive was concerned
because none of his/her team seemed to have any. Replies

from the panel were predictable – stop worrying about such silly things and start doing your job. Such things as charisma, after all, only exist in the mind.

They were half-right, charisma is not known as something you can touch, weigh or measure, and so it does only exist within us. However, it is not just in our minds, it is in our hearts as well. And there's the rub – if it exists in either, it is as real as we want it to be, therefore it exists. You know what I mean, you know people who have it, and people who don't.

I have been researching charisma for two years now, and I have reached the following three conclusions:

- **it does exist, and it is definable;**
- **everyone has it within them; and**
- **it is key to leadership, critical to Naked Leadership, now and always.**

A few months ago I received a leaflet for a one-day seminar, 'Charisma in a day' – great value at £99, excluding lunch. However, the blurb was the very ammunition that prevents us British from embracing such concepts of charisma as reality, rather than as some New Age fad that will come and go.

I define charisma as:

1. **Presence:** As opposed to absence. The invisible man lacked a certain presence. So be with your people, in person. Speak with them, listen to them, and show them they have value. Do this now, today and every day.

2. **Passion:** As opposed to indifference, and boredom. Is your boss boring? Do people yawn in front of you? You weren't

born that way – everyone wants to dance with life, to make their dreams come true. If your heart is not in it, find a new job. All leaders – all people, in fact – have to enjoy what they do to do it well, and others will notice if your heart isn't in it. And by the way, you can do something to put wow into your talks, zest into your style, and buzz into your presentations.

3. **Positive**: As opposed to negative. Anyone can be a leader when the seas are calm, it is during the times of greatest turbulence that true leaders emerge. Start to focus on what you and your team want, rather than what they do not want – on opportunities rather than problems, and on the now and future rather than the past – and you will become charismatic.

All three of these are defined by actions, behaviour and choice. Whether you have charisma is up to you. It is your choice.

Charisma comes down to self-belief. When we are certain about ourselves, and in ourselves, we radiate positive power to all that we meet. We do not have to speak to do this – it is something people sense. So the fast track to charisma is to be confident in all that you do. Note – this is not arrogance, it is the complete reverse, it is a self-certainty that we know, rather than one we have to go out of our way to show.

Charisma is a key component of true leadership. Every organisation has an enormous, latent force waiting to be released. Management will keep it stifled. Naked Leadership will set it free. And when it is free, everything else falls into place, automatically.

When you meet someone who practises charisma you

will feel inspired, yes. You will also feel warm, but above all you will feel your life has been touched by another. That is a feeling that is difficult to describe. The only word I can think of is magic. Maybe that could be the subject of another strategy clinic: 'Dear Expert, my Chief Executive lacks magic, what shall I do about it?' Maybe not.

They used to hold two-day courses in the US, which said they were about charisma. On day one they would tell you that you were useless, that everything you had achieved in your life so far had been a waste of time, and that you were a worthless, pathetic specimen of an individual. On day two they built you up again, to be all that you could be, and more. I once went on such a course, but unfortunately I couldn't make the second day.

If you wish to stay on Leadership of Skills, go to **Influence in Company Meetings** 14 (p97)
or
If you wish to change journey join **Leadership of Teams,** go to **One Team – One Voice** 37 (p241)

THE NAKED LEADER

your cv stands, or falls, for you

You have come from either:

17 'Integrity-based Networking' (Leadership of Career)
or
'Reverse Headhunting – Get Your Own Back'
7 (Leadership of People)
You are on Leadership of Career – 4 of 7

This is personal to your career – how do you make sure you are shortlisted for interview?

Answer: by making sure that your name, e-mail and paperwork leap to the top of the pile.

- Build a reputation and profile.
- A short, snappy and relevant cover note. One paragraph (maximum 50 words) on why you are applying – focusing on the top three qualities being sought, and how you have them in spades.
- Include a quote about you from someone else, a short reference. Being recommended by another is a thousand times more powerful than recommending yourself.

Then of course we come to the major influence – your CV. Make sure you have a WOW CV that stands out from the rest, and echoes three things, confidence, excellence and personality. Most CVs (95%) are:

- Too long (with too many trees suffering as a result).
- Faultless in track record (the best leaders of tomorrow have made mistakes, and learn from them).
- Boring (yes, be professional, but not totally mind-numbing – test: can you read your CV and be inspired?).
- Not focused on specific opportunities (scatter gun approaches fail).
- Brilliant at hiding the most relevant achievements (the proverbial haystack needle would be easier to find).

The ideal CV:

1. Absolute maximum two pages, ideally one (less is more, every time).

2. Start with a short biography about yourself – 50 words – written in the first or third person, this does not matter, but be consistent throughout.

3 Talk about your achievements, highlighting those most relevant, but also include lessons you have learned.

4 Make it interesting – include a section about you as a person – in the future companies will recruit far more on the basis of character than on competency.

5 Be persistent. Follow up every application with a phone call. It will show you are keen, and make sure your application is looked at again. Very few people do this.

6 Beware online services that do little more than process applications – when you phone, ask whether the person handling the position has inside knowledge of the industry.

The recruitment industry has always been a jungle, regardless of economic circumstances. For every position, you have one chance, so take it. Make sure you submit an application and CV that is easy to remember, as opposed to being hard to forget.

A recent survey for credit reference agency Experian found 71% of firms had encountered 'serious lying' on CVs.

This included people disguising a spell in prison as time spent backpacking, and graduates concealing a degree in case it jeopardised their hopes of a temporary job in a call centre.

The Institute of Personnel and Development says economy with the truth in CVs is an 'increasing problem'. 'The majority of job applications involve if not outright lies, certainly exaggerations,' says spokesman Nick Isles. 'These usually concern academic qualifications where there's widespread "grade inflation" – 2:2s tend to become 2:1s, that sort of thing.'

Salary is another favourite subject for those who 'impression manage' their CVs. 'People exaggerate their remuneration, maybe bumping up their salary by a couple of thousand, or treating things like pensions contributions as net earnings,' says Mr Isles.

'The third area where people often come unstuck is interests,' he continues. 'What they really like to do is put their feet up and watch telly with a can of lager, but this becomes translated into some exotic hobby or interest.

'The skill is walking the fine line between lying and making the most of the truth,' he says. 'That is the very secret of successful CV writing.'

(Source: BBC Online)

If you wish to stay on Leadership of Career, go to **Attracting The Headhunters** 38 (p245)
or
If you wish to change journey, join **Leadership of Skills,** go to **Charisma in a Heartbeat!** 12 (p89)

THE NAKED LEADER

influence in company meetings (boring or otherwise)

You have come from either:

12 'Charisma In A Heartbeat!' (Leadership of Skills)
or
'Oh, I've Had Such a Curious Dream!'
25 (Leadership of Company)
You are on Leadership of Skills – 4 of 7

Like it or not, much of our time, and energy, is spent in company meetings. We can make of these what we will – treat them as a waste of time and that is what they will become, use them to pass the time, and that is what they will do. However, utilise them to better understand your peers and organisation and to build rapport, and the time will not be wasted; it will be an investment, with some fun thrown in as well.

Many important decisions, directions and destinies are taken at meetings, boring or otherwise. So let us put aside those tedious aspects of organisational meetings, such as agendas, minutes and protocol, and focus on what's really important – the psychology of power at business and company meetings – so much can be learned without others realising that you are learning.

Much has been researched and written about behaviour, contributions and lessons of meetings. In research for this book, I decided to test some of these theories, both in and outside of organisations. These were tried out in meetings of over six people.

Which of these well known beliefs about meetings turned out to be true for me?

- **Sit to the right of a right-handed chairperson (or left of a left-handed) if you want to have greatest influence over him/her. Worked every time. There seems to be a natural tendency for the Chair to confide in/hold separate discussions with the person immediately next to their writing hand.**
- **Listen to what everyone says and then make your contribution. Sadly, no. I could not get a word in edgeways, as without exception people just spoke continuously. You may gain a greater understanding of what people want from the discussion, but you won't get your view across. There was one question I asked that did gain attention, in every meeting. You will discover this elsewhere on your journey.**
- **The funniness of jokes is directly proportionate to the**

seniority of the person telling them. Absolutely. When the CEO was present at one meeting he was always listened to in absolute silence, as if he was the sage of all subjects, everyone hanging on his every word. And when he made a joke everyone laughed. One could always tell it was a joke, because the CEO laughed first! When one of my friends offered a (far wittier) retort, no reaction from CEO, so no reaction from meeting.

Where you sit makes all the difference to your perceived contribution/relationship with the Chair. Half proven. They (whoever they are) say that if you sit directly opposite the Chair you will be in conflict, but if you sit at an opposite angle, you will gain greater eye contact and rapport. I sat opposite the Chair and looked indifferent, and in a different meeting sat diagonally opposite and smiled throughout proceedings. Both times my eye contact was ignored.

It seems to me that the way to master meetings is to have them sewn up before they happen, and that is more about the psychology of the individuals than the meeting itself. If you have gone to the trouble of speaking with, listening to and persuading the other attendees before the decision is taken, you will be on a firm footing for anything. How do you do this? Find out what they think/want by listening and asking questions, and make sure your solution/ recommendation fits their need. Simple.

How do you build rapport with people in meetings? There are many ways – eye contact combined with appearing to be interested works a treat (remember you only have to pretend), nodding also helps (but make sure you don't overdo it, and it is timed correctly). If you want to go further, read up about body language (now with the politically correct name of non-verbal communication).

But if you want to floor a meeting completely, wait until an acronym is mentioned, or some terminology or business process is referred to that you do not understand. If you do not understand it, chances are neither will anyone else. Then, in a clear, confident but slightly apologetic tone, ask what it means.

This worked brilliantly for me. Recently I was invited into an organisation by a chief executive who was about to invest a large amount of money in knowledge management. He was worried that the consultancy involved were not being clear about what benefits would come in return.

I sat in with the board of the company, listening to the consultant go on (and on) about knowledge management. Knowledge management this, knowledge management that. After a while I raised my hand and asked the sort of question that only people external to an organisation can ever ask.

'Excuse me, but what exactly do you mean by knowledge management?'

There was a long pause, and my heart beat three times faster than normal. Everyone in the room stopped writing and looked at the presenter. After what seemed like an eternity he replied. Looking me straight in the eyes with a look that could kill, he said:

'What I mean by knowledge management, David, is the management of knowledge.'

Silly me.

If you wish to stay on Leadership of Skills, go to
Awesome Presentations 48 (p307)
or
If you wish to change journey, join **Leadership of Culture,** go to **Leadership by Magazine** 31 (p205)

your team – from good to unstoppable

You have come from either:

27 'Your Personality Becomes Their Personality . . .' (Leadership of Teams)

or

49 'Leadership in Times of War . . .' (Leadership of People)

You are on Leadership of Teams – 2 of 7

People will only work their hardest when they want to. Carrots and sticks all play their part in encouraging this to happen, but unless people choose to deliver their best, they will simply not do so. To make this choice, people must identify closely with the culture, values and vision of their department, their organisation and each other. The deeper the identity, the more productive the relationship, harmony and bonding between a company and its people.

This inner sense of loyalty is hugely powerful in shaping the culture, success and very future of every department and company. When achieved, the benefits are extraordinary; way beyond high retention and excellent delivery, to a sense of community and purpose that knows no barriers.

Loyalty to each other is the most powerful antidote to office politics and blame cultures – when people realise they can be both accountable and make mistakes on their road to success. Learning from these mistakes is far more likely to happen when people help each other out, when they most need it.

At the heart of loyalty comes leadership. Leaders must set the example, and when they have done so, must live, breathe and act it through – when you do this, the loyalty of your people will be automatic.

Building such a loyalty-driven culture is not easy, but you owe it to the future of your company, your people and yourself to place it high on your agenda this year. All of the new technology in the world will come to nothing without the ideas, the drive and energy of people, and as a Naked Leader you have the power, the authority and the responsibility to help release it. Furthermore, when you genuinely believe in leadership – in supporting your people, and enabling them to be all that they can be – you will be allowed to make mistakes. We are all human beings, we all make mistakes, we all say things we later regret. People will still trust you when this happens, if they believe in your integrity.

There are many differences between being a manager and being a leader. One of the main ones is that a leader inspires loyalty based on who they are, and on what they do, not because of their job title or size of the office. People who work in such cultures feel such a bonding with their organisation that they could easily be working for themselves, in their own companies. That is true alignment. Build a culture that values all of your people, and places them at the heart of your department, and company.

- Begin by encouraging open and blame-free debate within your immediate team; draw out everyone's contributions, their hopes, fears and ideas for the future.
- Be a visible leader, talk and listen to people – learn their names off by heart.
- Consult widely, and put in place a set of values that everyone can identify with – include fun or happiness as one of them.
- Catch people doing something right and openly praise them; whilst you take personal responsibility for everything that goes wrong.

Those who put aside the traits and trappings of management and hierarchy, and become true leaders, will own the future. Forget Belbin and the other team-working fads and theories; it is when people work hard for each other that true, total and long-term teamwork is achieved. That is when people, and organisations, become an unstoppable force.

Frensham Heights School in Farnham is an extraordinary school, and is setting a trend that many organisations are beginning to follow. Their philosophy of individual free-dom (no school uniform, teachers on first name terms) within a clearly defined framework is the way forward for all teams. The headmaster, Peter de Voil, says:

'When I first meet new pupils and parents on their induction day, I address the pupils first, rather than their parents: I tell them they have a special contribution to make, as they bring with them a variety of different skills, talents and interests. I want to make each pupil feel that he or she is important and has a contribution to make that will be valued by the rest of the community. Once pupils arrive in the school, they are encouraged to take part, to share, to contribute – and will soon be aware that the school has a philosophy based on mutual respect, enthusiasm and enjoyment of each other's company and achievements.

'When pupils make mistakes or get themselves into trouble, they invariably find support from their peers, and not just the adults trained to support them. There is no prefectorial system but rather a peer mentoring system, whereby older pupils meet and talk to younger pupils in their classrooms once a week. This brings together two very different age groups and helps to break down barriers between age groups, which exist in some schools.'

Stantonbury Campus in Milton Keynes has an equally refreshing approach: 'What has not changed since [the campus opened in] 1974 is our deeply held belief in the equal value of all the young people we work with and our determined optimism about the potential of each one. We are justly proud of these principles and in the productive working relationships that they encourage. Positive behaviour is necessary for effective teaching and learning to take place and is itself an important outcome of education at Stantonbury.

In order to encourage positive behaviour, we aim to ensure the following: the provision of clear guidelines for student behaviour set out in a written Code of Conduct displayed in all teaching areas and in student planners, and regularly discussed with students; the establishment of warm, persistent and professional working relationships focused on the development of self-esteem, high expectations, achievement and positive behaviour; the provision of opportunities for success for all students in the classroom and through extra-curricular activities; the continuing development of formal and informal ways of recognising and praising individual and group achievements and contributions.'

If you wish to stay on Leadership of Teams, go to **Making Success So Easy to Achieve, and Failure Impossible** 35 (p229)
or
If you wish to change journey, join **Leadership of People,** go to **Reverse Headhunting – Get Your Own Back** 7 (p67)

ownership – who's in charge of you?

> **You have come from either:**
>
> **1** 'The Structure of Guaranteed Success'
> **or**
> 'People Mean Business – Improve Performance
> **45** By at Least 10% (Leadership of Team)
> You are on Leadership of Self – 1 of 7

If we don't take ownership of our lives, then someone else will. When things don't seem to be going our way, we have to be persistent, see the positive, or perhaps simply look in the mirror.

One very effective way to put this into fast practice is to write a letter to the single person who will play the biggest part in your success in the future. The person who owns your life. That's right – you. Write a letter to yourself about anything you wish – a commitment to achieve a specific outcome, how you feel about the future, or as a contract that in the future you will make different choices and decisions. Write it, post it and read it. It is an amazing experience.

Now, some stories of people who took true and total ownership:

Colonel Sanders. He was far from an overnight success story. When he retired, he had no money, only a chicken recipe. That's all, nothing else. So he decided to find a buyer for his recipe. He drove round the States, sleeping in his car, changing his ideas, always believing, and never gave up. He knocked on 1009 doors before he got his first yes.

Also, look at the stories of Sylvester Stallone, Billy Joel, Richard Branson, President Lincoln and thousands of others. And, closer to home, look at successful projects, businesses and companies that so nearly failed. Persistence is incompatible with failure.

We all see the world through different lenses, and we can choose how we see things. Two shoe salesmen from different companies travelled to a far-flung country to assess the market. After just a day, the first phoned back to base: 'They have never even heard of shoes here, let alone worn them . . . I am coming home on the next flight.'

The second also called in: 'They have never even heard of shoes here, let alone worn them... send me everything you've got.'

There are, it has been said, two types of people in the world. There are those who, when presented with a glass *that is exactly half full, say: 'This glass is half full.' And then there are those who say: 'This glass is half empty.' The world belongs, however, to those who can look at the glass and say: 'What's up with this glass? Excuse me? Excuse **me?** This is my glass? I don't **think** so. **My** glass was full! **And** it was a bigger glass.*

(*From* The Truth *by Terry Pratchett*)

Finally, it is our own behaviour, positive or negative, that determines how effectively we build and maintain rapport.

A monk lived a quiet, reclusive life in the hills, just off a little-used track that connected two distant villages, one in the north, the other in the south. Occasionally travellers would pass, and he would always invite them in to share some time, food and conversation. One day, a tired looking man called in on his way from the north. He was exhausted, unfriendly, and made short, sharp efforts at exchange: 'Tell me, monk, what are the people like in the village to which I travel?'

The monk replied: 'Before I answer, tell me, how did you find the people in the village from which you've come?'

The traveller said, 'It was a horrible, unfriendly place. The people made no effort, and I hated my time there.' To which the monk replied, 'In which case, I must tell you that you will find the people in the south much the same.'

Two days later another traveller arrived, much fleeter of foot, and of a far happier disposition. He asked the monk about the people in the village ahead, and the monk asked the same question about those he had met in the north.

The traveller said: 'The village I have come from was a wonderful place, a real community. People made me feel so welcome, they shared their stories, their food and their hospitality. They became some of my closest friends, and I was sad to leave.'

To which his host replied: 'In which case, I must tell you that you will find the people in the south much the same.'

Each of these stories can be labelled 'positive thinking'. This concept has had a bad press from many people (usually negative thinkers), and of course positive thinking in itself will not change the world, it has to be combined with decisions and action.

However, in itself it is a massive start, and it has been proven that positive thoughts actually enhance our health – not surprising really, given that stressful ones clearly do not help us.

Feeling positive about yourself makes you healthier. There are all kinds of research for this. For example, some researchers analysed quotes from top team baseball players in the US over 50 years. The results were stunning: the optimists – those who were quoted as believing in themselves – lived significantly longer lives than the pessimists who put their success down to luck. Confidence. In the US again, patients were divided into three groups before undergoing serious spinal surgery. One group were told that they could focus on removing blood from the spine, and then returning it after the operation. The second group were taught relaxation techniques, and the third left alone as the control. The first group, who had been advised that they could control their blood flow, on average lost half as much blood as the other two groups. This is proven stuff – optimism is good for you.

Positive thinking does not mean avoiding the harsh

challenges of life, it does help put us in a more resource-ful frame of mind, or state, to tackle them. I once led a programme of cultural transformation in a big company; a magazine did an interview and article about us, they headed it, 'Happy smiley people'. Oh dear!

There once was a rich businessman in London who had twins. And you know how babies have a personality almost from the moment they are born? One baby was miserable, the other was happy. And it continued all the way through their early childhood – everyone remarked on it, but their father refused to accept it. He decided to test it out once and for all on their tenth birthdays. In the small hours he filled the pessimist's room full of the most amazing toys and presents you could imagine. And the optimist's he filled full of horseshit. Early the next morning he crept past the pessimist's room. He could hear him grumbling, 'This won't last long, I didn't really want one of these.' Then he went to the optimist's room – and he could hear him whistling a merry tune! He burst in the door to see his optimist son whistling away shovelling horseshit out of the window with a spade:

'Why are you whistling when your room is full of horse-shit on your birthday?'

'Hey Dad, with this amount of horseshit, there must be a pony here for me somewhere!'

* * *

Nasrudin was at the fair with his followers when he decided to give them a demonstration of his archery. All of them watched as he drew his head back in a military manner and took careful aim – only to miss the entire target with a wild shot. The onlookers began to snigger, but Nasrudin turned round and said, 'That is how a soldier shoots, wildly and inaccurately, in the face of the enemy. I said to myself as I took aim, "Nasrudin, you are a soldier" and this is the result!'

Intrigued, the crowd waited for his next shot. With his second arrow he merely tweaked the bow and the arrow fell twenty yards short. 'Now,' he said, 'You see the shot of a timid man who muffed his first attempt and was too nervous to make good with the next.'

Then he turned again before anyone could speak and fired an arrow that hit dead centre in the bulls-eye. As he carried off his prize one of his followers clutched at his sleeve and said,

'But who was shooting then?'

'Ah,' said Nasrudin, 'that time it was **me!**'

If you wish to stay on Leadership of Self, go to **Jargon Free NLP!** 22 (p141)

or

If you wish to change journey, join **Leadership Company**, go to **Organisational De-structures** 18 (p121)

THE NAKED LEADER

integrity-based networking

You have come from either:

5 'The Power of Mentoring' (Leadership of Career)
or
'Making Your Strategies as One' (Leadership of
39 Company)
You are on Leadership of Career – 3 of 7

Many leaders ask me what is the most important success factor in personal and career achievement, and the answer I always give is the same, networking. Identifying, establishing and developing your relationships with other people is a hugely powerful way to develop yourself, and others.

Networking takes effort, it takes time to build up close contracts both inside and outside an organisation, and time is a precious commodity, so networking must be carefully managed for maximum benefit. However, it need not be a struggle, we crave human interaction, it is simply the lack of hours in a day that dictates our need to approach this activity in a structured, professional and focused way.

The benefits of networking are:

- **Visibility/profile**: A critical factor in successful leadership, and the more visible you are, the higher your profile.
- **Awareness**: Keep your ear to the ground, to the grapevine (which operates across industries as well as inside companies). Grapevines are simply giant games of Chinese Whispers.
- **Learning**: We all have a great deal of knowledge, skills and wisdom to share with, and learn from others.
- **Camaraderie**: A feeling of togetherness, the social interaction that is so vital to our self-esteem. It is a natural craving we all have, and share.
- **Achievement**: So much more can be achieved with other people, and the feelings of success are far greater.
- **Power**: In many organisations, communities and industries, whom you know plays a bigger role than what you do. This may not be fair, or politically correct, but it is reality.
- **Reputation**: Combined with your other activities and successes, your reputation will travel around by word of mouth – the ripple effect is amazing. However, make sure you build a reputation to be proud of.

One very important element of business and social inter-action is, of course, our natural desire to help others. It is only through human interaction that we can find out others' hopes, fears, dreams and desires. Above all else, I advise anyone serious about widening their professional and social circle to do it on the basis of what they can offer other people and their organisations.

Everyone has already established a network, perhaps without realising it. The challenge is to focus on, and spend time with, those who will help us achieve our aims, while ensuring we help them in equal and greater measure. These people should be identified – what are their aims? If you do not know them already, how can you meet them?

The simplest ways of widening your network is to attend conferences, seminars and peer groups. Once you have established contacts and built rapport, make sure you keep in touch with people. There is a true saying – help others while you are on the way up, as you may need them on the way down, so maintain your network way beyond any reasons for initial contact.

Some important tips:

- **Never compromise your values or beliefs.**
- **Always be there when someone needs your help.**
- **Keep your word – at all times.**
- **When someone takes you into their trust, never abuse it.**

Our busy and hectic lives dictate a disciplined approach to our lives. Building rapport, trust and ultimately total loyalty is a powerful, long-term asset for anyone, and it is by doing this that you will widen your circle of professional colleagues.

In our lives, we can help people we network with, friends and strangers, in so many ways. One way is through random acts of kindness. Pay for the car behind you at a toll bridge, stop and speak with a homeless person, or just make a decision, in any moment, that puts another person before yourself.

And some tips for when you first enter a meeting, or any room where you do not know people:

1 *Walk boldly into the room standing tall and poised as if on a mission.*

2 *Pause a little way inside the door (clear space) in a confident manner and look for friends or friendly faces (as if you are looking for someone).*

3 *If you get some eye contact from someone in a clearish space in the centre of the room (preferably someone you know, but this is not essential) then just go directly over to them.*

4 *If not, head for a group of three people (avoid two together, more difficult to break in) – and hover.*

5 *During a break in the conversation, introduce yourself. Or if a third person is not involved, introduce yourself to him/her.*

6 *Do this by making direct eye contact, shaking hands and saying 'Hello, I'm xxx, and I am . . .' (have a one-liner ready that describes you). The other person will introduce themselves.*

THE NAKED LEADER

7 KEY POINT . . . *Your next line should be a question relating to something the other person/other people have said in their introduction.*

That's it – you're in.

If you wish to stay on Leadership of Career go to **Your CV Stands, or Falls, for You** 13 (p93)
or
If you wish to change journey, join **Leadership of Company,** go to **Hidden Account Management** 34 (p221)

organisational de-structures

You have come from either:

39 'Making Your Strategies as One' (Leadership of Company)

or

16 'Ownership – Who's in Charge of You?' (Leadership of Self)

You are on Leadership of Company – 2 of 7

One of the big fads of the last ten years was so called 'flat structures'. Business Process Re-engineering combined with the age of empowerment to wipe out organisational hierarchy forever, streamlining the decision-making and communication processes to ensure faster, flexible and more focused action.

If only! The reality delivered something rather different. Indeed, our attempts to achieve democracy and more power to our people by erasing reporting lines has left a legacy of issues, among them:

- Large numbers of people reporting in to one person.
- Confusion of who owns what.
- An increase in dotted line reporting – resulting in unclear accountability (one chief executive I know calls this 'dotty line' reporting, which says it all).
- Similar projects happen with different accountability – promoting confusion not cohesion.
- Muddled succession planning.

Otherwise, simply eradicating reporting lines was an outstanding success!

These results have left many companies with literally the wrong shape to face and embrace the new business age that is now upon us. The fast-moving, opportunity-laden and exciting new world of change, the Internet and e-business calls for clear ownership, leadership at every level, and a culture of action and automatic innovation.

As a leader in the new millennium, what can you do to ensure your team, department and company catch up, and overtake present and future needs?

- Become a true leader, when job titles and structures matter little compared with your personal style, attitude and actions – key test, if you were stripped of all of your trappings of status, would you still get the best from your people?

- Turn your department upside down by announcing that

you report to everyone in it, your prime role being to bring out the best in them.

- Ensure clear ownership and accountability – regardless of who reports to whom.

- Where you have dual reporting, only one person should be responsible for leadership and direction, and one for work accountability.

- All of your processes and procedures should be centred on your customer, internal or external, and must allow for ideas to thrive, and actions that drive forward.

- Put in place a clear set of values.

Lines drawn on pieces of paper, job titles and hierarchies are an integral part of any organisation, large or small. If we focus on and try to erase them, on their own, without replacing them with a new culture of leadership, they will simply come back again – people need the security that such structures bring.

However, it is the mindset that is critical. Regardless of whether you have fourteen levels, or one, make sure you have in place true empowerment, where people know what they are there for, and are able to make decisions accordingly. Focus on an outcome where every activity in your company is directly related to a result that gains or retains customers, motivates people or increases revenue, and where the culture has a buzz of activity about it, rather than a frozen stagnation. Then you will be moving forward, driven by a rediscovered community based on being human, as opposed to being able to draw straight lines, dotted or otherwise.

People often confuse structure with power. I was once delivering a leadership programme to 40 people in a team, ten each week for four weeks. At the first session I asked the first ten how many of them believed that hidden agendas played a part in the team of 40. They all put their hands up. I then asked who in the room had a hidden agenda. No one put up their hands. Ah-ha, it must be the other 30, but no, after the third session, no one had their own hidden agenda, so it must be the final ten. No, no one there either!

Hidden agendas mean different things to different people. To me, they simply mean your own agenda, your own thoughts and feelings, and most of these are bound to be hidden!

If you wish to stay on Leadership of Company, go to **Job Evaluation in the Bin** 6 (p61)
or
If you wish to change journey, join **Leadership of Culture**, go to **Balance The Sources of Power** 11 (p85)

THE NAKED LEADER

room 101

You have come from either:

31   'Leadership by Magazine' (Leadership of Culture)
or
33   'Modelling' (Leadership of Skills)
       You are on Leadership of Culture – 7 of 7

If you have tears, prepare to shed them now, and some other things as well!

What would you consign to the fires of hell? And remember, I said *what*, not *who*! We have only a few moments, and 500 words, to destroy forever our biggest obstacles, challenges, and hassles . . . so let's get burning

10 All those useless manuals from the training courses you never did anything with. I know they stand as a testament to your policy of lifetime learning, but be honest, have they also led to lifetime action? Your shelves were beginning to buckle under their sheer weight anyway, and will be hugely grateful.

9 All those posters hanging around the office telling us all to be motivated, and to take a pride in our work. True motivation comes from within, not from an A3 cartoon character . . . if you can't burn them, hang them upside down . . .

8 Reserved car parking spaces for 'Executives'. A great way to demonstrate equality and openness. However, when you decide to do this put a five minute time limit on the discussion, or it will go on for hours. Come on, you've got a company to run!

7 Drinks machines that pretend to be so sophisticated they can store 500 different varieties . . . when we know that whatever we press we always get the same muck! Dispense with them now.

6 Invitation to tenders on anything. It is sadistic to force suppliers to fill out the damned things – no one even reads them, let alone bases any decisions on them! (Supplier contracts just survive, as we need something to take home for our children to draw on.)

5 All TLAs (three letter acronyms), in particular BPR, of course – also anything beginning with ISO; it's all good, combustible stuff.

4 Competency assessment forms. Replace them with a dart-board. Actually, on second thoughts, file them – in a year you will cry with laughter at the way we used to measure talent, skill and human potential with a multiple choice, emotional quiz.

3 Your office. Be visible . . . It is not only the way of Naked Leaders, it is also the fastest route to that magic thing called charisma. Strip it down and do it today – we need the wood to keep the flames alive.

2 Service level agreements. No one really cares how your service teams perform, it is their perception of how they think you are performing that counts. The days of boring, percentage-based performance statistics are dead forever.

1 Annual budgets. Anyone still doing them is living in the last century. We simply cannot plan more than three months ahead, if we are to be fast, flexible and fit enough to survive in this new business age.

That should clear out a lot of paper, unnecessary work-load, and frustration. And, by the way, before you write in, while I say burn, I do of course mean recycle. After all, over the last few years, isn't that what our companies have perfected – to the art of genius?

By the way, do take some care what you reject and throw away . . . it may well reappear to haunt you!

- *Ronald Reagan was rejected for the lead in* The Best Man *in 1964 because they thought he didn't look enough like a president.*

- *William Orton, CEO of Western Union, turned down and dismissed Alexander Bell's offer for the exclusive patents to the telephone saying: 'What use can this company make of an electronic toy!'*

- *'Groups with guitars are on the way out' – Decca man Dick Rowe, turning down The Beatles.*

- *The author of* The Power of Positive Thinking, *Norman Vincent Peale, was so depressed and negative about his manuscript that he threw it into the wastepaper bin. It was rescued by his cleaning lady and went on to be a best-seller.*

You have completed Leadership of Culture, go to
Enlightened Leadership 42 (p263)
or
If you wish to change journey, join **Leadership of People**, go to **Our Secret Driving Forces** 3 (p45)

THE NAKED LEADER

doom or disaster,
welcome to neg-land

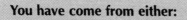

You have come from either:

7   'Reverse headhunting – Get Your Own Back'
(Leadership of People)
or
'The Power of State – Everyone Needs a
29   Place to Be' (Leadership of Self)
You are on Leadership of People – 7 of 7

The CEO, and board-level peers, are important power
bases for you to be aware of, and act on. However, there
is a force nearer to home that demands equal, and just as
urgent, attention. It is a group of people who make any

CEO look like your best friend. Collectively, they have the ability to bring others down, to radically change our careers and, at an extreme, to destroy your team.

I am, of course, talking about . . . the negs. Or internal terrorists, as some prefer to call them.

We all know who the negs are; they are the people who love to find something, anything, wrong with an idea. They will always point out (with great glee) how things will not work, and are doomed to failure. Every company has them. Taken as individuals they are little more than a disparate group of unhappy individuals who skulk around in corners, moaning behind our backs. Together they form a powerful, collective force of negative energy.

As you read this you may be smiling, pondering on some specific names and people who come within this category. Smile no more, they are the disciples of doom and gloom, they are a virus, and they must not prevail in our teams, departments or companies. I am not suggesting their views are suppressed, or that we all walk around being positive and optimistic for no reason – rather that people's views must include, from time to time, some constructive suggestions and alternatives. That is the important distinction between negativity and objective contribution.

As Naked Leaders we have to put aside the option of negativity and an outcome of failure. We have to put in place a compelling vision based on success and achievement.

It is time for us to apply constructive, creative and positive energies so that we can move forward. We must start to achieve steady, stage by stage progress.

We can do that through openness – listening to and involving people. This is the ultimate neg antidote – asking them their opinion in public (after all, they complain behind your back, all the time, about never being noticed or listened to).

By involving people you will achieve their buy-in and support. The negs will have no excuses, as their most powerful argument is that they are never consulted or involved.

As leaders, we must also put in place a compelling vision for our department and our people. The negs cannot cope with open leadership, or a positive future.

The disciples of doom have had it their way for too long – it is time to stop them. Involve and encourage them – if they don't play ball, then take them on. Just leaving them to one side does not work – they will ambush you when you least expect it.

Focus on a powerful, positive and passionate agenda in your department and the negs will fail. Those that are not converted will crawl back under the rocks from which they came. Hopefully they will leave you; if they do not, you must simply part company with them. You cannot allow the negativity of a few to drag down the positive visions of the many. The negs must fail, for you to succeed.

By the way, the most powerful way to confront a neg is as follows:

Approach them at their desk, ensure there are other people (witnesses) present. Remember that negs thrive by telling others that you never pay them any attention, or ask their opinion on anything. You are about to disprove this. Make idle chat, not just with the neg, but with the group of people around him/her. Raise a subject about which you know the neg has an interest, or skill, or is involved with in their job. Then, warmly ask for their thoughts on a particular aspect of this. It is brilliant, because they cannot announce they have no thoughts! I have done this many times, and many negs have turned around and complained about me to my face, which is exactly what I was seeking!

When negs reach positions of power they often become bullies – business bullying is becoming a big issue in organisations. If you are ever bullied – my definition is if anyone says or does something that worries or frightens you, verbally or otherwise – tell someone senior, and tell them now.

Bullies, and negs, are often people who are crying out to be valued. To anyone who does not feel valued, who feels lonely in their place of work or in their life, or feels they have little to give, I offer these life-changing words:

'Our worst fear is not that we are inadequate. Our deepest fear is that we are powerful beyond measure.'

'It is our light, not our darkness that frightens us.'

'We ask ourselves: "Who am I to be brilliant, gorgeous, talented or fabulous?" Well, actually, who are you not to be?'

'You are a child of God.'

'Your playing small doesn't serve the world.'

'There is nothing enlightened about shrinking so that other people won't feel insecure around you.'

'We were born to make manifest the glory of God within us. It is not just in some of us – it is in everyone.'

'And as we let our light shine we unconsciously give other people permission to do the same.'

'As we are liberated from our own fear our presence automatically liberates others.'

A Return To Love by Marianne Williamson,
HarperCollins (1992)

(By the way, these words are often incorrectly attributed to Nelson Mandela.)

You have completed Leadership of People, go to
Enlightened Leadership 42 (p263)
or
If you wish to change journey, join **Leadership of Self**, go
to **The Fastest Way to Make Any Change In Your Life** 30
(p195)

following the lines and breaking the rules

You have come from either:

1 'The Structure of Guaranteed Success'
or
'A Leader's Biggest Timewasters' (Leadership of
4 Company)
You are on Leadership of Culture – 1 of 7

I was once given detention at school for turning my English notebook on its side and writing across the printed lines. It was unacceptable, as my English teacher said, 'Why do you think the lines were there in the first place?'

I would love to meet him again. Indeed, leaders, teams and organisations are vying with each other to write across the printed lines – the new rule is to be the first to break the rules. All rules are to be challenged (broken) – except this one!

Follow these 'lines' with care . . .

1 Business process re-engineering (BPR)

The sell: Come with us and re-engineer your services, business and company. We will improve all of your processes, save money and make you more efficient.

The purchase: The vast majority of projects failed. BPR focused on processes, not people, on secret downsizing rather than openness and honesty, and on cutting costs rather than attracting new business and customers.

2 Job descriptions

The reason: All roles and responsibilities must be defined, along with the skills needed to do them.

The dangers: Organisations are not in the paper business, they are in the people business. Job descriptions have a place (in the bin), but if you have them, make sure they are flexible, provide individuals with freedoms to move around and develop, and focus on deliverables, outcomes, rather than just ongoing tasks. Instead, consider having 'people descriptions'.

3 Ideas schemes

The big idea: Let's look within our organisations to find the ideas that will save us money, make us more profitable and more effective. So, we will seek out the best ideas and reward people for them.

The small challenge: Ideas are great; awakening the innovation, insight and imaginations of people are keys to success. However, ideas schemes must avoid simply pointing fingers at other teams, or areas of a company. And they are worthless unless they happen. Make sure that you have the abilities to make them real, fast.

4 Competency-based anything

The cunning plan: We'll identify a set of criteria against which we will measure people and how they are doing. We may even link it to their rewards. Also, we'll use this to identify people's weaknesses, for people to work on during the following year.

The flaw: We all have different strengths, skills and talents. When we do not work with these, they weaken. 'Competency' – perhaps the most boring word to ever come out of our HR departments – does not engender excitement. Competency-based anything brings in the concept of empowerment; and that in itself is a problem. It is simply not possible to 'empower' people, as we are naturally empowered. It is only possible for organisations to disempower.

5 Total quality management (TQM)

The theory: This team will focus on quality, and everything we do will be of a set, minimum standard. We will do things right first time, avoiding expensive repetition and saving time.

The reality: The problem is that it can take you five years getting something absolutely, totally, perfectly 'right', and even then it may prove to be 'wrong'. TQM can freeze people into fear of doing anything, in case it is wrong.

6 Continuous improvement

This is priceless: Every day we will get better and better, by doing the things we do well, ever so slightly better. In this organisation we believe in evolution, not revolution.

This is worthless: Where's the excitement, the passion, and the step change everyone is seeking? It's a jungle out there and only the fittest, fastest and most flexible will survive and thrive.

7 Best practice

The investment: Let's spend cash to find out what the industry has found out to be the best, risk-free way to do something, then let's do the same.

The cost: Let's do the same things that many others have already done and ensure that, while we may make fewer mistakes, we will forever swim in the sea of conformity. Instead, identify those pioneers that have broken away and are shaping the future, and do what they did (modelling).

Chaos can be fun, and excellent for business. I was at a conference that was opened by a CEO who bemoaned not knowing what the future held.

'I used to know what my turnover would be, I used to be able to predict the behaviour of my customers, I used to be able to know what would happen next, and it is so depressing.'

Audience in tears, I felt like doing a quick whip-round for him as he didn't look like he had eaten for a while.

The next speaker was also a CEO.

He started the same, and reached a different conclusion:

'I used to know what my turnover would be, I used to be able to predict the behaviour of my customers, I used to be able to know what would happen next, and it is so wonderful. By not knowing what the future is, it means I can shape whatever future I want.'

I recounted this story to a school – and ended my talk on a crescendo of how exciting it is to work in a world where no one knows what will happen next. Suddenly a hand went up at the back of the room, and a boy said:

'I know what will happen next sir, we've got double French.'

If you wish to stay on Leadership of Culture, go to **Values-based Leadership** 32 (p209)
or
If you wish to change journey, join **Leadership of Career**, go to **Attracting The Headhunters** 38 (p245)

jargon free NLP!

You have come from either:

16   'Ownership – Who's in Charge of You?' (Leadership of Self)

or

3   'Our Secret Driving Forces (Leadership of People) You are on Leadership of Self – 2 of 7

NLP stands for Neuro Linguistic Programming.

The aim of this book is to strip away the hype, and so, until now, I have not referred to NLP in its own right for three reasons: NLP is full of jargon, hype and complexity, it is itself not original, and its founders have lost a lot of credibility through legal disputes.

However, NLP does bring together many ideas and practised theory under its umbrella.

Welcome to the NLP jargon free charts. Here are the top ten NLP tools and techniques, presented in reverse order of personal impact. And I repeat again, NLP does not 'belong' to anyone, it belongs to everyone.

10 **Remove emotions by observing the emotion itself, not judging whether that experience is 'right' or 'wrong'. So, next time you feel angry, say to yourself, 'Ah, this is anger.' The very act of observation gives you greater control.**

9 **Try to touch the plus sign:**

+

You have probably touched it now – but that is touching it, not trying to touch it. Trying is a dangerous word that throws us into confusion – you will either do something, or you will not, and we often use 'trying' as an excuse. Replace the word 'try' with 'do'.

8 **If you want to give up a bad habit, but you do not, it is usually because that habit gives you some pleasure. Identify what that pleasure is – be honest with yourself, then ask yourself how you could achieve this same pleasure doing something different. If so, you will be on the way, because you will not be 'giving-up' the pleasure, you will be replacing it. If smoking gives you the pleasure of relaxing, and you find that meditation gives you the same pleasure – meditate. (You can meditate in more places than you are allowed to smoke!)**

7 **Change the way you talk to yourself. Many people believe the happiness in your life comes down to how you**

communicate with yourself – your internal dialogue. Think of phrases you enjoy hearing, and repeat them silently to yourself throughout the day. No one else need know you are doing this, except you will have a huge, knowing grin, and feel fantastic.

6 Change your perception of a past event by picturing it in your mind, making it smaller and then turning it into black and white. Enhance a positive memory by bringing it closer to you, and placing yourself in the memory, as opposed to just observing it.

5 Visualise a task that you have to do, but which you dread, such as doing the dishes. Then think of an image of you positively LOVING doing the task. See the first image as a large picture, with the second image as a smaller one, placed in any corner of the bigger picture. Now SWAP the images, replacing the first with the second. Repeat ten times. Enjoy those dishes!

4 Mirror other people's behaviour – one to one. They cross their right leg you cross your left. They lean on their left hand you lean on your right. Keep doing this in a discreet way, in the course of the conversation. Then, after a while, make the first move, perhaps by rubbing your chin – if they do the same (i.e. rub their chin, not yours!) you have established rapport. It is amazing.

3 Ramp up positive emotions by using words like sensational, awesome and orgasmic, and reduce negative emotions through words like peeved, miffed and mellowed. Next time your partner upsets you say that you feel 'slightly grazed' – the emotion is less, immediately.

2 Put yourself into an unstoppable state (standing tall and breathing deep, feel like a tree, with roots securing you to the ground). Put on inspiring music that means something wonderful to you. Now, close your eyes and touch your thumb and first finger together of your dominant hand. Repeat this ten times. Every time you touch your thumb and first finger together in this way you will recreate that state of mind and feel unstoppable.

1 Finally – most powerfully – people think with a mixture of pictures (visual), sounds (auditory) and feelings (kinaesthetic). Everyone has a dominant pattern. You can tell what this is, and whether someone is lying to you, as follows:

Ask a question and watch the way the person's eyes move. It will reveal their most dominant way of thinking, and whether they are remembering something, or making it up (constructing).

Question 1 – 'What was the colour of the candles on your 12th birthday?'

Their pupils move . . .

- up and to the left (their left) – visual remembered;
- to the side and to the left – auditory remembered; and
- down and to the right – kinaesthetic feelings.

Question 2 – 'If you could wish for anything in the world, what would it be?'

Their pupils move . . .

- up and to the right (their right) – visual constructed;
- to the side and to the right – auditory constructed; and
- down and to the left – kinaesthetic internal dialogue.

Build faster rapport with visual people by using phrases

such as 'I see what you mean' or 'I get the picture'. With auditory say 'Sounds great' or 'I hear what you are saying' and with kinaesthetic 'You'll simply love this' or, 'How does that make you feel?'

And of course, now you will know if anyone else is lying to you . . .

Much of NLP is about focusing all of your senses on what is happening to you, around you and within you, at any moment in time . . .

Ellen Brown summed this up like this:

'I wish I could enjoy events as they happen, rather than just watch events pass by. Like most people I have spent many years working long hours and travelling to far flung places to be "a success". I believed it was possible to be the superwoman – successful business woman, mother, wife, home maker, cook, hostess, friend?? But the reality is there are simply not enough hours in the day to "do it all" and there is very rarely any time left for me. The work life balance hasn't always been equal, and work usually had the larger portion. I do believe it is possible to address the balance and I have started to do so. I have realised that the material possessions success brings are nice to have, but only if you have time to enjoy them.

And from Bill Parslow . . .

'I cycle to work every day. Every day I get down to the seafront and stop just to take a breath of fresh air and look at the sea and sky. It might be for a few seconds, but it is enough. OK I'm lucky, you say. But no, I commuted

1¾ hours to London for 7 years in all – and like all big cities, there's a large river running through it. Walking over London Bridge the sky and the river open up around you. It is a fantastic vista, a moment to be enjoyed. Wherever you are, walk for at least 15 minutes in your city, town or village, and look up. Amazing cloud changes, new sky-lines and buildings – just drink them in. And spare a thought for all those people passing by – I guarantee that 95% will have their eyes fixed straight ahead or on the ground in front of them.'

If you wish to stay on Leadership of Self, go to **The Power of State – Everyone Needs a Place to Be** 29 (p183)

or

If you wish to change journey, join **Leadership of People**, go to **Leaders Are Born and Not Made!** 10 (p81)

recapture the magic . . .

You have come from either:

32 'Values-based Leadership' (Leadership of Culture)
or
28 'Project Success' (Leadership of Teams)
You are on Leadership of Culture – 3 of 7

Go into any new company, one that is just starting out. Witness the enthusiasm, energy and excitement as the founders discuss their dreams, shape their future and make their plans a positive reality. Feel the culture of a new project at its launch – a new team comes together for the first time, full of hope and expectation at the success ahead of them. Experience a company as it grows fast; see the ideas, instinct and imagination flow through everyone involved, like a collective heartbeat of inspiration. It is a healing process, providing an atmosphere of certainty in the destiny that is being shaped by constructive forces.

Go into any large company, one that has been established for a while. Introduce a management initiative, call it total quality anything, or continuous improvement, or worse still, business process re-engineering, then stand back and watch. The blame starts slowly at first, then grows, fast. It eats its way through an organisation, freezing new ideas, initiative and action in its wake. It is like a virus of negativity. War breaks out as everyone focuses on saving costs, avoiding failure, and rooting out anyone who dares to make a mistake. It is a harming process, providing an atmosphere of inevitability in the disaster that is being shaped by destructive forces.

It is no one's fault of course, rather a harsh reality – when organisations reach a certain size they stop looking at how to expand, and auctioning ideas that will drive the company forward, and instead start to look at cost savings, process improvement and efficiencies.

Most of these companies have forgotten why they exist, and have certainly lost sight of any sense of compelling destiny. Their corporate imagination becomes totally utilised in survival through mistake avoidance and problem solving. People become scared to make any decision, take any actions, and conformity becomes all-pervasive. The positive spirit that was present all those years ago has died, and the soul of the company is black.

These are the companies that said you can never sell insurance over the phone, that direct banking was sure to fail, that shouted with pride that no one would ever make money over the Internet.

It will be organisations that drive forward with a positive, compelling and visionary agenda that will thrive in the future. And their spirit will soar.

Everyone talks about cultural transformation. Academic tomes have been written on the subject. The question is: are you brave enough to do it, in reality?

Real cultural transformation requires openness, honesty and trust, and can only be developed by throwing out the traditional culture of blame, and investing time in building a positive, transformed environment.

This is the antidote to negativity, and it will dramatically increase staff loyalty, motivation and retention.

Cultural transformation means different things to different people and what works in one company may not in another. It is important to set your own transformational agenda, and to focus on the issues and needs in your environment.

A good starting point is to revive, review and restate your organisational objectives. Ensure they become a set of deeply held beliefs that guide you towards meeting your aims while trusting and respecting each other.

Involve everyone in deciding a code of ethics and values for the future. This will help secure ownership and commitment across the whole team. Be consistent – if, as their leader, you once stray from these values, you risk losing your followers.

Values such as openness, trust and loyalty are usually high on the list for companies who have started on this exciting path. One I worked with recently even included fun, and why not? In many departments people seem to be actively encouraged to leave their personalities, and sense of self, at home in the morning.

Combine this with widespread and sincere effort to

encourage and develop people through coaching and support. This will promote involvement, real empowerment and personal growth by strengthening people's inner belief systems and self-confidence.

These are some ways of starting towards the aims of cultural transformation, to create a community of purpose where people enjoy work, where they utilise their talents to best effect because they want to, and where they are recognised and rewarded for the contributions they make.

Cultural transformation addresses the very heart and soul of a team, department or organisation. It is a prerequisite of success in the new global economy, where our people are our only unique currency.

When successful, the rewards – personal, team and corporate – are enormous. It can, however, be a dangerous path – for such action, although most people and companies know it is the right thing to do, is still very rare. It calls for thinking way beyond the old management competencies of planning, organising and control. It calls for visionary thinking, persistent resolve and a laser focus on success. Above all else, it calls on you to become a true leader – the big question is, are you ready to step forward and make that difference?

How your team perform, and are perceived, in your organisation depends more on the identity, attitudes and behaviour of your people than on any other single factor. It is time to liberate their aspirations, their potential, and to ignite the human spirit.

The Invitation

by Oriah Mountain Dreamer

It doesn't interest me what you do for a living. I want to

THE NAKED LEADER

know what you ache for, and if you dare to dream of meeting your heart's longing.

It doesn't interest me how old you are. I want to know if you will risk looking like a fool for love, for your dream, for the adventure of being alive.

It doesn't interest me what planets are squaring your moon. I want to know if you have touched the centre of your own sorrow, if you have been opened by life's betrayals or have become shrivelled and closed from fear of further pain! I want to know if you can sit with pain, mine or your own, without moving to hide it or fade it, or fix it.

I want to know if you can be with joy, mine or your own, if you can dance with wildness and let the ecstasy fill you to the tips of your fingers and toes without cautioning us to be careful, to be realistic, to remember the limitations of being human.

It doesn't interest me if the story you are telling me is true. I want to know if you can disappoint another to be true to yourself; if you can bear the accusation of betrayal and not betray your own soul; if you can be faithless and therefore trustworthy.

I want to know if you can see beauty even when it's not pretty, every day, and if you can source your own life from its presence.

I want to know if you can live with failure, yours and mine, and still stand on the edge of the lake and shout to the silver of the full moon, 'Yes!'

It doesn't interest me to know where you live or how much money you have. I want to know if you can get up, after the night of grief and despair, weary and bruised to the bone, and do what needs to be done to feed the children.

It doesn't interest me who you know or how you came to be here. I want to know if you will stand in the centre of the fire with me and not shrink back.

It doesn't interest me where or what or with whom you have studied. I want to know what sustains you, from the inside, when all else falls away.

I want to know if you can be alone with yourself and if you truly like the company you keep in the empty moments.

If you wish to stay on Leadership of Culture, go to
Balance The Sources of Power 11 (p85)
or
If you wish to change journey, join **Leadership of Teams**, go to **Making Success so Easy to Achieve, and Failure Impossible** 35 (p229)

THE NAKED LEADER

skills of leadership
over management

You have come from either:

1 'The Structure of Guaranteed Success'
or

8 'Synchronicity' (Leadership of Self)
You are on Leadership of Skills – 1 of 7

The world of the traditional manager reminds me of a good sea Captain. His or her life dictated by external factors – the weather, the sea, and the passengers. He can never be in command of these forces, but he can always remain in control of how he reacts, behaves, and leads.

It seems to me that leaders can live an easier life, and take control of their own future, by learning and putting into practice a certain set of skills.

What are these skills, the characteristics of tomorrow's great leader? Combining all of my work to date on leadership, these are the top seven skills offered by delegates . . .

① Wider vision: The new leader will have in place a compelling future for their people and department. Involving others in its formation, they will keep it shiny, relevant and focused on achievement.

They will have a wide perspective – combining strategic business knowledge with a clear view of, and involvement in, their industry/market and its direction. They will be the first to see strategic opportunities outside their organisation and combine this with an ability to illuminate the most complex of these to their business colleagues, board and CEO.

② Personal profile: They will have a very high profile and visibility. Daily walks through their department and regular 'open forum' style meetings will be high on their priorities. They will know everyone's name off by heart, and take a genuine interest in people's thoughts, concerns and interests.

Successful future leaders will have that mysterious factor often referred to as charisma – combining a friendly nature with positive energy and a dynamic personality. They will hold their heads high and be proud of what they do, while still maintaining great humility, sense of humour and an attitude that brings out the very best in others.

③ Warrior: One of the main characteristics of a future leader will be his or her ability to make it happen – to take action and lead by example. They will take risks, confident in the results and greater rewards. They will make mistakes and take blame, but will ride this out in the belief and certainty of their overall direction and vision.

The warrior rarely accepts credit – preferring instead to pass such praise on to their people. They are, however, a mover and shaker. They will have the ears of the chief executive and be seen, first and foremost, as a successful businessperson at the heart of the organisation.

They will also play the high stakes game, recognising that politics are rife within each and every company. They enjoy being at the cutting edge of such organisational games – playing to ensure recognition and success for their people and department.

4 **Alliances and friendship**: Being a leader can be a lonely existence, and personal and departmental success cannot be achieved by one person alone. The future leader will form powerful alliances with other companies, directors and external groups to achieve mutual aims. Suppliers will be trusted partners, helping the internal department achieve their goals.

Knowing they do not have all the answers, leaders work hard on personal development, combining this with external guidance and advice. They will also have identified, and be close to, the real power players within the organisation, keeping their friends close, their enemies closer.

5 **Spirit – higher self**: Successful leaders are at one with themselves and have their lives in balance. They combine an energetic spirit with a sense of priority and perspective, and know how to relax.

They have a persistence to deliver and succeed, and a

deep-rooted self-confidence and self-belief that transcends adversity – taking responsibility for things under their control and for their reactions to events they cannot control.

6 **Imagination and mind skills**: Working to develop an already razor sharp mind and, recognising the power of people's ideas and contributions as the most powerful factor in success, ensuring that creativity thrives.

They do not allow their department to get bogged down in company initiatives that have no clear direction. Instead, they ensure that they create an open culture where ideas flourish – the more unusual and bizarre the better.

7 **The ability to inspire**: The new leader does not have an office – and earns respect and trust based on who they are, what they do and what they stand for, not from their job title, what they say or their hierarchical position in the organisation.

They accept that they are accountable to their people. They will have a leadership promise in place that lists the specifics and spirit of that commitment – what people can expect of him/her, how quickly e-mails will be responded to, etc.

Many refer to these new dimensions as 'personal power' – a combination of attitude, belief and behaviour. It is within all of us to take this path – it may not be the easiest, it will certainly involve leaving comfort zones, but it is the most rewarding.

A leader is a person – a leader is you or I – and if we choose to we can achieve the most powerful benefits and results that anyone could ever imagine. Are you ready?

Gareth Brown, who understands emotional leadership better than anyone else I know, talks of the acid test of leadership: if you were stripped of your title – the power to punish and reward your people – would you still get results out of them?

Would you?

As Gareth says . . . 'the new Leaders know that real and lasting power comes from within. When we learn to lead from the "inside out" we naturally become more powerful and therefore more inspirational to others.'

It is this ability to inspire others that differentiates the great leaders. But how can we become more inspirational? Is it something we can learn? Gareth recalls his own personal experience:

'I remember a time early in my career when I was trying to understand what it would take to be more inspirational as a Leader. After reading numerous books, listening to countless tapes, and attending a multitude of seminars I was still at a loss, unable to find any real answers.

'Then, one day, as I was out for an early morning run, the little voice inside my head asked "What inspires you?" "Mountains," I replied, and continued running.

'That evening I was reading a book by Lene Gammelgaard, a Danish mountaineer who had climbed some of the world's highest peaks. She had been one of the survivors of the Everest Tragedy of 1996 in which eight people had been killed.

'Gammelgaard's book contained an afterword that was a tribute to a friend of hers called Anatoli Boukreev. He had also survived the tragedy, only to be killed later in the year whilst climbing in the Himalayas. The following quote by Boukreev resonated with me and reminded me of my earlier internal conversation.

"I would like to believe that the roads we choose depend less on economic problems or political problems or the imperfections of our external world, and more on our internal calling, which compels us to go anew into the mountains, to the heights beyond the clouds, making our way to the summits.

"The sparkling summits and the fathomless sky above our heads, with their grandeur and mysterious beauty will always draw humanity, which loves all that is beautiful. This was, is and will be the magnetic strength of the mountains, independent of the worldly, trivial vanities and fusses, beyond which, at times, we cannot see the real, the beautiful and the eternal."

'It's clear that the mountains inspired Anatoli Boukreev, calling him to look beyond the imperfections of the external world and to see instead **the real, the beautiful and the eternal**.

'Unlike Boukreev, I realised that the mountains that I climb are not always real in the physical sense; rather they are a metaphor that represents the highs and lows of my life's challenges. Like his mountains however they call me forth, compelling me to reach for new heights that always exist beyond the clouds of self-doubt.

'Inevitably it is this inner calling – the quest to find the real, the beautiful and the eternal in ourselves and others – that serves as the only true source of inspiration.

'I know that when I am in touch with this source I too, like the mountains, seem to possess a magnetic strength that attracts others, inviting them to climb with me in search of another "sparkling summit".

'Nowadays I make a point of climbing real mountains too. They remind me that no matter how steep or difficult the path I have chosen if I just keep moving one step at a *time I will eventually arrive at my destination.*

'I notice also that as I climb my personal horizon expands and I regain a broader perspective. What seemed difficult or worrying suddenly seems easier and more manageable. And when I reach the top I am once again able to see the breathtaking beauty of the world in all its glory and splendour.

'When I return from my climbs I am left with a sense of connection to something greater. I feel more calm and peaceful. I become more energetic and tackle challenges with enthusiasm and relish. I become more passionate and determined. I feel better able to inspire others because I am myself inspired.

'In his book No Ordinary Moments, *author Dan Millman sums up my experience perfectly:*

"Your path will lead you over some lofty peaks and down into some dark forests. From each peak, you'll see the bigger picture and feel on top of the world and closer to God. Down in the shadows of the forest – your own shadows – you'll confront necessary challenges and discover the strength within you. So both the highs and lows are useful in their own ways."

'I believe that as the new generation of Leaders we have many metaphorical mountains to climb. There are many challenges to be faced and no doubt many of us will stray into the dark shadows of the forest.

'It will take enormous personal strength and courage to move through the shadowy times and search once again for the sparkling summits. It will require Leaders with tremendous insight and vision. Leaders who are prepared to serve as an inspiration to others and who are prepared to look for the real, the beautiful and the eternal in everyone they meet and in everything they do.

'Remember . . . if you want to become an inspiration to others you have to first become an inspiration to yourself.'

If you wish to stay on Leadership of Skills, go to **Building Total and Absolute Rapport** 41 (p257)
or
If you wish to change journey, join **Leadership of Company** go to **A Leader's Biggest Timewasters** 4 (p49)

'oh, i've had such a curious dream!'

(*Alice in Wonderland*, Chapter 12)

You have come from either:

4 – 'A Leader's Biggest Timewasters' (Leadership of Company)
or
30 – 'The Fastest Way to Make Any Change in Your Life' (Leadership of Self)
You are on Leadership of Company – 7 of 7

A business director, James Palmer, once told me about a dream he had. As with many leaders who have major problems on their hands, James always slept like a baby – waking up on the hour, every hour.

In his dream, James was in work as normal, until he was

visited by the senior partner of the consultancy firm they had been using on one of their major projects. The work was nearing completion, and the partner had requested a meeting. He knew perfectly well in advance what it would be about – the consultancy would want to extend their contract, and would use every trick in the book to do so.

The consultant walked in, they shook hands and James put on his negotiation hat. The consultant spoke first:

'Thank you for agreeing to see me, Mr Palmer. As you know the project we have been assisting you with is coming to an end. General opinion is that it has been an outstanding success, and I just wanted to thank you for using our company, and to let you know that, as long as you are happy with our work and contribution, we will be pulling our people out a week on Friday.'

James was so taken aback he simply stammered out something like, 'Fine – thank you,' and shook the partner's hand. He did make a mental note, however, to make sure he used this company again.

He needed fresh air, but before he had a chance, his phone rang. It was his chief executive officer. James braced himself, and put on his grovelling hat. The CEO said:

'Good morning James, I hope you are well.'

'Very well, thank you, eh, Vince,' James replied.

'Great – just a quick call to say I received that new sales report from your department last night, and it is absolutely brilliant. It tell me everything I need to know, and I just wanted to ring and say well done.'

The phone went down, and before he could be interrupted again, James left his office and headed for the door. He walked quickly around the car park, the only fresh air alternative being a five-mile drive away. However, soon he was not walking alone, he had been joined by Claire, the HR director.

'Keeping fit, James?' Claire enquired.

'It has been a strange morning – I am just gathering my thoughts,' James said.

'I'm glad I caught you, anyway', Claire continued, 'This new corporate initiative – Total Quality . . .' she paused as James put on his angry hat, '. . . we've decided to dump the whole thing, along with Continuous Improvement and all the ideas schemes. They cause far more problems than they are worth, and actually had the effect of reducing ideas and effectiveness, rather than enabling it. In future all company schemes will have to pass a clear cost-versus-benefit analysis at board level before we even consider them.'

And with that she said goodbye and walked inside the building.

James was beginning to enjoy his day now, strange as it was. However it looked like taking a distinct turn for the worst when he met the claims director, Adam Michael, at the coffee machine. Adam was the business manager in charge of a major project that had just gone off the rails – late, over budget and no prospect of delivery.

'Ah, James, I've been looking for you,' Adam began in hushed tones, James put on his defensive hat, 'I wanted to have a quiet word with you about the project. As you know I am the business owner for the project and, no matter what the cause of the problems, as owner I am taking full and total responsibility for the problems, and resolving them.'

James looked at him in silence. Adam walked away as he uttered the last words: 'There is no point being accountable for something and not owning up when it goes wrong, is there?'

James sipped his coffee, and made his way back to his department. He decided to call in at the help desk to say hello. It was an area under great pressure, and he wanted to raise their morale. The help desk supervisor, Mike, greeted him: 'Hi James – how are you today?' Before James could put on his morale-boosting hat, Mike continued: 'This has been a great day James, everyone who has called us has been really polite and understanding. They seem to know that the problems they have are not our fault, and that we are here to help.' James stayed for half an hour and, sure enough, the atmosphere supported Mike's comments. His team were going about their business, answering the calls and helping their customers.

As he returned to his office, James saw a visitor waiting for him outside. His heart sank, she was from a supplier that James had agreed to see because the company had talked about 'guarantees' and 'shared risk'. 'Now that she has made it to my office,' James thought, 'let's see if she remembers those words.'

After exchanging the usual pleasantries, James decided to be very direct: 'Diane, when we spoke on the phone, you said that you would share the risk on this project, what did you mean by that?' There was a pause as Diane seemed to struggle for a reply. James put on his killer hat, for the first time that day. 'Got you now,' James thought, 'today may have been the most amazing I have ever had, but some things never change – suppliers would never put their money where their mouths are.'

The silence seemed to last an eternity, until Diane spoke at last: 'Yes, Mr Palmer, yes indeed. That is exactly what we will do – our company will undertake to resolve the issues you face, and be paid strictly according to the results we achieve. If, at the end of the project, our product does not deliver what we say it will, you may have it completely free of charge.'

The silence that followed was far longer than the first. And then, for the first time in over six months, James put on his happy hat. 'That's strange,' he thought, 'it feels just like a pillow.'

Grow Great by Dreams, *author unknown*

The question was once asked of a highly successful businessman: 'How have you done so much in your lifetime?' He replied, 'I have dreamed. I have turned my mind loose to imagine what I wanted to do. Then I have gone to bed and thought about my dreams. In the night I dreamt about my dreams. And when I awoke in the morning, I saw the way to make my dreams real. While other people were saying, "You can't do that, it isn't possible", I was well on my way to achieving what I wanted.' As Woodrow Wilson, 28th President of the US, said: 'We grow great by dreams. All big men are dreamers.'

They see things in the soft haze of a spring day, or in the red fire on a long winter's evening. Some of us let these great dreams die, but others nourish and protect them; nourish them through bad days until they bring them to the sunshine and light which comes always to those who sincerely hope that their dreams will come true. So please, don't let anyone steal your dreams, or try to tell you they are too impossible. Sing your song, dream your dreams, hope your hope and pray your prayer.

* * *

'All men dream: but not equally. Those who dream by night in the dusty recesses of their minds wake in the day to find that it was vanity: but the dreamers of the day are dangerous men, for they may act their dreams with open eyes, to make it possible.'

T.E. Lawrence, The Seven Pillars of Wisdom

You have completed Leadership of Company, go to
Enlightened Leadership 42 (p263)
or
If you wish to change journey, join **Leadership of** .
Culture, go to **Influence in Company Meetings** 14 (p97)

THE NAKED LEADER

succession planning

You have come from either:

38   'Attracting The Headhunters' (Leadership of Career)
or
40   'Our Next Generation' (Leadership of People)
You are on Leadership of Career – 6 of 7

Future leadership is your responsibility. You owe it to yourself, your team and your company to identify and develop future leaders, in particular ensuring that you have invested in your replacement.

Forget old fashioned succession planning, in which you sit down with your HR Director, pen and ruler in hand, and draw straight lines with names on it. This is far more fundamental than that. It is the deeply personal action of creating a vision of the future, and making it happen.

Most of us avoid doing this, for understandable reasons:

- **We do not know the skills our organisation will need in the future**: A sound argument for doing nothing – but as few of us can confidently predict the next three months, let alone years, it must be overcome. In the leadership domain the skills, knowledge and behaviours needed in the future are the same as those that true leaders display right now.

- **There is no one immediately identifiable for such consideration**: This is probably because the subject has taken a back seat in the past. Far from being a reason for inaction, this is a strong argument for fast decisions and investment in key people to rectify the situation.

- **We feel threatened by grooming our next-in-line**: This implies that we become more indispensable if there is no one to replace us. Cloud-cuckoo-land! In today's business world your prospects depend upon how well you leverage the talent, energy and creativity of those who work for you. Never make your organisation dependent on you; it is a false security that will backfire.

- **The company will recruit externally**: All teams need new faces. However, this is expensive, uncertain and it takes time. If we fill too many key positions externally, what message is being sent to our own high-flyers?

In reality, high-quality leadership skills are not widely

available. As more companies rely on external recruitment the overall position will worsen. Trained people will simply not be available, and departments will be forced to promote staff who are not ready.

We often bemoan the lack of skills available within our own companies, while slashing costs of training at budget time. Because a company's survival, growth and destiny depend on its people, and particularly on its leaders, we simply must invest in the new generation.

We should scour our departments to identify future leaders at every level. Create a programme for your fast-trackers and make sure they are looked after, so they will stay with you as they continue to grow. By making this investment, you will be doing more to secure the future than anything else you could do.

When you decide to move on you will be judged by the strength of assets you leave behind. What will your legacy be? A successful project, a piece of infrastructure, or a dynamic new leader carrying your flag, ready to take on the world?

How do you want to be remembered?

Your true value lies within you . . .

There's a story about the chairman of a large international, say BP, who was out driving with his wife one day, in the area where she grew up. When they stopped for petrol he noticed his wife looking hard at the petrol pump attendant – and the attendant returning the look in a slightly embarrassed sort of way. As they drove out he said: 'Did you know that man?' 'Well, yes,' she said, 'he was one of my first ever boyfriends, way back in school.' The chairman chuckled – 'I can see you thinking how if you married him, you'd be the wife of a petrol pump attendant – aren't I right?' 'No,' she said, 'actually I was thinking that he would have been the chairman of BP.'

If you wish to stay on Leadership of Career, go to **The Five Pitfalls of Leadership** 46 (p293)
or
If you wish to change journey, join **Leadership of Company**, go to **Making Your Strategies As One** 39 (p249)

your personality becomes their personality . . .

You have come from either

1 'The Structure of Guaranteed Success'
or
44 'The Choice of Opposites' (Leadership of Skills)
You are on Leadership of Teams – 1 of 7

Your character, style and behaviour have a huge impact on your people, and team.

People in your company are right now crying out for guidance, leadership and direction. They are ready and willing to give their best – but unsure what to do, where to go, or whom to trust.

The incredible power that one person, or a small group

of people, can have inside an organisation is not often appreciated. They influence the motivation of others, the culture in their team (often clones of themselves) and, above all, the effectiveness and results of their department.

Have you noticed, for example, that the personality of managers and leaders has a habit of permeating throughout the department? At one extreme there are those who are dynamic, visible and visionary, on the other, those who are passive, never seen and obsessed with detail.

Clearly there are many shades between, but these fundamental extremes demonstrate the difference between doing a job of management, and being a leader.

Leadership is an evolving role, no longer about pioneering, more about the ability, and desire to inspire, enable and encourage others to achieve their true potential.

Naked Leaders realise that being stuck in a big office is not the best place to appreciate what is really going on – they ensure their front line are free to make all the decisions they need to make.

Naked Leaders are not comfortable being perched on top of a contrived hierarchy – they turn hierarchies upside down, and invest their time in supporting their people.

Above all, true leaders do not rely on position or job title. They earn respect on the basis of what they are, the values and behaviour they demonstrate in reality.

Many refer to these new dimensions as personal power – a combination of attitude, belief and behaviour.

Every organisation has an enormous, latent force waiting

to be released. Management will keep it stifled, leadership will set it free. And when it is free, everything else falls into place, automatically.

I call on all leaders everywhere: release the incredible power that exists inside your organisations – by influencing just a handful of people, who will in turn inspire others, you will start a ripple effect that will release the creativity, innovation and potential of many, many more.

Once upon a time, in a company not very far from here, the finance director, Charles, was preparing for Christmas as he had always done, with dread, despair, and depression. He hated Christmas, and everything that went with it. He did not believe in giving Christmas cards, waste of money, and those he received he never opened, storing them instead in a pile in the corners, on top of his unopened copies of business magazines.

And this day would be the worst – firstly he would have to go outside of his office to visit his 'people'. He had no wish to do this, but a memo from HR had suggested that in future, managers should be more 'visible'. Then it was a boring Christmas party, in which people who spent the entire year sending hate e-mails to each other would suddenly pretend they were everyone's best friend. Finally, it would be time to go home. Home to his empty and cold house to spend the holiday on his own – he had no family, and no friends.

It was midday when there was a knock on his office door. It was a woman he did not recognise – probably chasing up the pound he still owed to Children in Need. She entered and, without invitation, sat down.

'Can I help you?' he asked her. 'No, I am here to help you,' the strange looking woman replied. He decided she

must be from marketing. There was a long pause. The two sat in silence, looking at each other.

'Can we do this by e-mail?' The finance director broke the silence. 'I am a ghost', the woman said in a matter of fact tone. 'Very nice, have you seen a doctor?' Charles replied, realising this must be a practical joke.

'I am the ghost of Christmas past, present and yet to come,' the woman persisted, 'and I am here to take you on a journey.' 'Aren't there supposed to be three of you?' 'Yes, but your budgets were slashed so badly this year you couldn't afford more than one.'

And before he could say any more – it was twelve months earlier, and they were in the middle of the general office. Everyone was rushing around, panic everywhere.

'What are they doing?' asked the woman, now strangely floating six inches above the desks. 'They are doing last minute preparations for the budgets', Charles replied, now looking fearful. 'And what happened as a result of their efforts?' the woman asked – 'did these people not help keep this company afloat – and what thanks did they get?'

'They got their bonus,' the finance director replied in disgust. 'MONEY – is that all you think about – they are screaming out to be motivated, for inspiration, for leadership.'

The lights flashed off and on – Charles was now on the floor of his own office, surrounded by people who were laughing. 'You are invisible', the ghost whispered – 'open your eyes and your ears to what goes on around you, every day.'

Charles lay very still, wondering what to expect next – he listened to his team talking.

'I can't wait until he's gone – what a misery.' 'Look at those cards – he hasn't even noticed I've given him the same one every year.' 'Just look at the size of this office – you could fit six of us in here.' 'He hasn't come past the tide mark since last Christmas.'

As if anticipating the question in response to this last remark, the ghost pointed down at the floor, where a small piece of white tape, almost invisible, was stuck to the carpet.

'Your people put that down a year ago, it is a mark of how far you come out of your office during the day – your staff never see you, many of them don't even know who you are! Now I have to go. It will be your choice whether I come back next year.'

There was a loud clap of thunder, and he was not in the office anymore – he was in the company boardroom, surrounded by his peers. He was a year in the future – and the other directors were angry, shouting at him. He could not make out what they were saying, other than the occasional words:

'Demotivated . . .'

'Cost . . .'

'No leadership . . .'

He tried to defend himself, he began to make excuses, but no one was listening. The shouting increased in volume, until he could take it no more – 'ENOUGH!' he screamed, 'enough.'

And then they were silent, and he was back in his own office. He clutched onto his desk to make sure it was real . . . yes it was. He rose slowly and opened his door. Glancing down at the small white tape with a smile, he walked out of his office, into the open area. No one looked up, even though he was coming out further than he had ever done before.

Charles paused next to one of the desks, he picked up a

phone. *'Hello, is that Premises department, could you spare one of your people please, I have a private office that needs to be removed.'*

If you wish to stay on Leadership of Team, go to **Your Team – From Good to Unstoppable** 15 (p103)
or
If you wish to change journey, join **Leadership of Career**, go to **The Power of Mentoring** 5 (p53)

THE NAKED LEADER

project success

You have come from either:

43   – 'Project Leadership' (Leadership of Teams)
or

2   – 'Living as a Leader' (Leadership of Self)
You are on Leadership of Teams – 5 of 7

Projects run organisations, and can ruin them, as well. We manage them every day and so often they go wrong. All projects would be in a far healthier state, with more delivered on time, to budget and really meeting the needs of a company, if they all had a clear business owner. There should be no such thing as a specific departmental project, everything an organisation does must lead to an agreed, stated and measurable benefit.

Just imagine if all projects had clear, visible and accountable owners, prepared to ensure success, and take action to avoid failure. Ready to carry the mantle when timescales start to drift, without immediately resorting to blame and backstabbing.

Such work often begins with the best of intentions. The outcomes and results are clear, business leaders within the company are clamouring for a piece of the action, to be associated with something new, dynamic and exciting. The team is formed, pictures taken for the in-house magazine, morale is high. Slowly and surely, events start to go wrong. A missed milestone here, a new cost there. Soon key people are not available for specification and training, and people begin to wonder why the work was started in the first place. The bright new vision has been lost forever.

Most projects are destined to fail from the moment the premature, confused and lacklustre go-ahead is given. How do we break this cycle, and ensure real business ownership, and ultimately higher rates of success?

- **Every project must have a clear company owner, riding all the challenges as one, and maintaining ownership throughout.**

- **Team cohesion and leadership must be the top priorities.**

- **The more mission-critical the project, the more senior its business owner should be.**

- **Each piece of work must have a real tangible benefit – if it can't be put in a wheelbarrow and delivered, the project should not be started.**

● **Benefits must be delivered on completion – that must be in writing on day one.**

● **When the going gets tough, revisit and restate the big picture. Too many people working on projects do not get a share in the vision.**

There are too many project failures. Get this. In the last ten years, the UK Government's IT projects have lost at least £5 billion; that's over £5 billion of our money. How many hospitals is that? Those that fail invariably do so because of bad planning, budgeting or management. As leaders we owe it to our organisations to put in place clear owners, who are strong, focused and ready to work hard. Please go out now and review your projects, and create more business heroes, and fewer invisible men and women.

You have thought about the critical skills you need around you in projects. Please take a few minutes to write them down:

....

....

....

....

....

....

....

....

....

Exactly.

First step: *Never, ever refer to the term 'softer' skills, call them the 'critical' skills.*

One IT/Business leader who understands both the need for, and impact of, these skills is Tim James, of Legal and General. As he says:

'A short time ago I was asked to define the way forward for a major e-commerce opportunity. There were several different perspectives of how the proposition would develop, but I had to home in on just one. Time was against me, as it often is in the early stages of a project, so I had to take the lead and work out whether this opportunity could have real business or justify closing it.

'I pulled together a small, but highly skilled, cross-functional team. Briefing and coaching them in equal measure was vital to get more than one brain working on the solution. As our vision became clearer we checked back regularly with the business owner and with other interested parties to make sure their needs and perspectives were considered. Where they were excluded, careful negotiation, careful influencing or a recrafting of the vision was required.

'We got the approval for the initiative within 4 weeks and successfully built the business proposition during the following year. This could have been one of many projects. It called for leadership, team building, coaching, influencing, communicating and negotiating. Just like all the others.'

If you wish to stay on Leadership of Teams, go to **One Team – One Voice** 37 (p241)

or

If you wish to change journey, join **Leadership of Culture**, go to **Recapture the Magic** . . . 23 (p147)

the power of state – everyone needs a place to be

You have come from either:

22 – 'Jargon Free NLP!' (Leadership of Self)
or
– 'Job Evaluation in the Bin' (Leadership of
6 Company)
You are on Leadership of Self – 3 of 7

In your final moments on this earth, how many of you will look back on your lives and say, 'I really wish I'd spent more time in the office.'

Our state is defined as how we feel, at any moment in time. As right now is the only moment we are actually living in, our state becomes a critical factor. If we are worrying right now, in this moment, we will be in a disempowered state. If we are enjoying the moment, we will feel 'happy'.

State changes happen fast, usually triggered by external events – an aggressive e-mail, sometimes just seeing someone's name in our 'in-box', that certain look from a business colleague, or the car that overtakes us to reach the traffic lights first. All of these can have an impact on our state.

Many human potential and success books have been written on state, often making it sound at best a mystery and at worst a four year psychology thesis. The fact is that we can alter our state whenever we choose. It is, quite literally, our choice.

There are many ways to do this, three of the most powerful being:

1 **By taking control of how we react to external events**

2 **To ramp up, or down, the emotion**

3 **By finding our perfect place of balance.**

1 Taking control of how we react to external events

When the boy racer accelerates out of the side road, causing us to swerve, there are unlimited ways we can react. However, at the time, our feelings, our state, kicks in and we do something we may later regret. It seems at the time that we only have one possibility open to us, whereas, just two hours later, when we look back at the event, perhaps being slightly more detached from it, we see there were other alternatives.

Adrian Gilpin, chairman of The Institute of Human Development, talks brilliantly about a 'gap' – a moment of time between an event happening and our reaction to it, or action because of it. There has to be a moment, albeit brief. And it is in that moment that we make our choices. Imagine the possibilities if we can extend that gap, imagine the number of choices we can then make.

And we can. The most effective way to extend the gap is to spend time in it. And we spend time in it through relaxation and meditation.

2 Ramping up, or down, the emotion

When we have an experience we enjoy, a special moment, we find that by giving it our total and undivided attention, by being right in the centre of the experience, we feel the moment more. In his wonderful book, *The Power of Now*, Eckhart Tolle describes the absolute joy that is available to us by fully immersing ourselves in each and every moment – in effect, to 'be' in the moment 100%.

When something happens that causes us upset, or we have an experience that does not serve us, we can do the complete opposite. We can distance ourselves from the event, by taking the emotion out of it. Think about a recent time when you were upset, now replay that in your mind, but take out all of the emotion, and emotional judgements, that you made. In the boy racer example it might be:

'I was driving along Farring Road, and a red sports car pulled out in front of me. It was going fast. I had to brake to avoid a collision, and I carried on driving along Farring Road.'

Still not a pleasant experience, but now perhaps a much more objective assessment than previously, when the number of expletives themselves would take up two paragraphs.

3 Being Centred

The most natural state of being is one of absolute calm, total tranquillity and inner peace. Reaching this state comes entirely from within. We may hold external events accountable for our state – e-mails, the rain, our family – but we have everything we need to be at one with ourselves, within us. Think about martial arts – their primary teaching is one of balance, oneness with the moment, so they are in the absolute peak state to handle anything that happens, in that moment.

So, as in martial arts, why not in life? And you don't have to dress up in baggy clothes to reach such an awesome feeling of peace.

When we are centred, in any areas of our lives, we are truly living in the now. We are focusing simply on the present moment (a powerful time to focus). We also feel a perfect balance, and sense of self-worth and control.

The very centre of our selves – where our mind, body and spirit come together, is physically located about one and a half inches below the navel and one and a half inches inward and toward the spine, is the point of the body's centre of gravity – its balancing point. In our lives we are surrounded by complex and impersonal forces that seem to be beyond our control. If we give in to these forces and allow them to dominate us, our life will be just a cycle of tension, pain, and frustration. Being centred enables one to find quiet, peace, and calm within our-selves in the midst of this turmoil. It is the point within ourselves that gives us mental and physical balance, allowing us to experience the ultimate sense of harmony with the universe. This is the reason that this area is focused on during breathing exercises and meditation.

Our Centre is a most important physical point, espe-cially for physical activity, as it is situated in the middle of the body and is the vital mid-point which balances the upper and lower portions of your body.

Its importance within the martial arts lies in the con-sideration of the balance you achieve through focusing on it. The first thing a karate student learns is the relationship of his/her body and mind.

And we know when we are centred – when we are in total and absolute control of our self. Remember there is no 'right' or 'wrong', there is only what helps us move closer to where we want to go and what takes us further away. It is clearly your choice (as ever) to be centred, or not. The question is, would it help you to feel in control of your life, or not? (Although you may think this is a very obvious question, I believe it is an important one. If you answer it in a clear and concise way you are more likely to put this into action in your life).

So – when can being centred most help you? It's not a question of 'how', it is a choice of when.

Place any thoughts you have in Your Centre and you will feel more in control of them. If they are causing you some worry at present, Your Centre will both give you greater command of them, and enable you to make wider choices about what to do. If those thoughts are already positive, place them there and their beauty, joy and warmth will grow.

Start by putting your hands on Your Centre – place your right hand on your front, so that your belly button sits just above your thumb – this is Your Centre. Now place your other hand on top of your first.

Begin with a minor worry. Think about it, and feel the slight discomfort that this gives you. Now, give that thought a physical, identifiable shape, of your choice. Let's say you have chosen a small silver ball.

In your mind, let the ball move from your head, see it move down through your neck, past your chest, and down into Your Centre.

The silver ball now rests in the very centre of your being and as it rests there it shines. It glows with an energy that runs throughout your body like a warm river of power.

Note – Your Centre is located very close to the stomach. Our worries and greatest fears rest in this area. As you move your thought down you will pass through the stomach – it is important to keep the thought moving through so it reaches and rests in Your Centre. If after this exercise the worry is greater than before, it is in the stomach. Simply move it that little bit lower.

You will know when the thought has reached Your Centre. You will quite simply feel in total control of it. It will not go away (at some stage you may have to address this issue, so we do not want it to go away), and you will be in a much better place to deal with it, in a far more empowering way.

Your Centre is the most powerful place in your body. Just as if you take a worry there, you will feel more in control (and therefore *be* more in control) so if you take a positive thought there, you will feel even more positive about it – you will feel wonderful.

Your Centre is there to serve, and it does no other. It will do this throughout your life, any and every time, on whatever subject and at whatever time you choose. And it is completely private – you need tell no one else. They may be able to tell, however, as you will glow.

Your Centre is an amazing 'anchor' (jargon term for holding onto a particular state, and accessing it whenever you wish – and by the way, when you decide to do this, you 'launch' your anchor!!!) It is with you all the time (portable), it is discreet and it is very personal to you. However, if that is not enough, next time you take yourself into Your Centre, when you are in it, make a deliberate action with your hand (you can remove it from your body for this), such as making a fist. From that moment on, every time you make that movement, you will automatically recreate the same feeling.

You will have discovered what it means to be a human *being*.

However, as we juggle meetings, phones and endless paper, it is easy to forget that we are human *beings*, not human *doings*. The great irony here is that we would actually be far more effective if we took some time out for ourselves. Everyone knows it, many now write about it, few put it into practice – the way to take command of your life, to achieve your best on a consistent basis, is to relax, and recharge.

Our energy is a finite resource, and technology was meant to make our lives so much easier. It was supposed to simplify the way things are done, to eliminate paper and to free up time. It has done the exact opposite, accelerating the pace, pressure and complexity.

Stress is one of the biggest issues facing leaders in the 21st century. From a leadership and director's point of view, it is disturbing; from a personal point of view it is damaging.

Stress has an antibody, called relaxation. The most powerful, proven and positive way to not only reduce stress, but also to recharge your energy, is to take some time out for yourself.

Relaxation has many advantages:

- Improved health, levels of energy and self-confidence.
- The great irony of its approach is that when people do this on a regular basis they are more effective in all aspects of their lives, including at work!
- It is also totally private to you and your family if you wish to share it with them.
- It takes very little time.
- It is free.
- It is totally natural – no matter what the rush-rush life around us may suggest!

The most powerful, immediate and effective method of relaxation is to do this:

1 Allocate 20 minutes every day;

2 Find a peaceful place, sit quietly, and upright;

3 Pay attention to your breath – only to your breath; and

4 Each time you notice a thought, allow your attention to return to the breath.

Do this, with variation – find out what works for you – for 21 days, and you will feel very different. Over time you will condition yourself to be able to relax more easily, perhaps in your office, or on the train.

In a remarkably short period, you will find yourself with more energy throughout the whole day – enabling you to spend so called 'premium time' with your family, and not just at work.

When we relax we do not enter a new world; we merely access a world that is already present, but that has been long buried. Some call it meditation; it goes by many names.

Meditation is a set of attention practices leading to an altered state by expanded awareness, greater presence, and a more integrated sense of self. Meditation is one of the proven alternative therapies. It can be broadly classified under the mind-body medicine. Meditation is a safe and simple way to balance a person's physical, emotional, and mental states. It will benefit everybody.

Doctors prescribe meditation as a way to lower blood pressure, improve exercise performance in people with angina, help people with asthma breathe easier, relieve insomnia and generally relax the everyday stresses of life. During meditation, the body gains a state of profound rest. At the same time, the brain and mind become more alert, indicating a state of restful alertness.

There is scientific evidence that meditation can reduce blood pressure and relieve pain and stress. When used in combination with biofeedback, meditation enhances the effectiveness of biofeedback. 'Through meditation one can learn to access the relaxation response (the physiological response elicited by meditation) and to be aware of the mind and the way our attitudes produce stress,' says Dr Borysenko, author of *Minding the Body, Mending the Mind*. 'In addition, by quieting the mind, meditation can also put one in touch with the inner physician, allowing the body's own inner wisdom to be heard.'

Above all else, remember it is OK to spend time with yourself. You are allowed to be at ease. It is the most natural state on earth.

In the world of sports the importance of an optimum state is well known. Indeed, athletes consider it a precondition to winning.

Strange, this does not follow through to our personal lives; but it can, and it works. Runners will focus, breathe deeply or find their Centre at the start of a race.

We can do the same, anytime we choose. We do not have to be fit, and the beauty is that we do it inside. It is private, totally discreet. You simply have to decide when you wish to make it happen, and I promise that when you do you will feel, and be, totally alive – at one with your-self and everything around you.

So, you can either do this right now, or not.

To me it comes down to whether we were born to live, or to prepare to live.

* * *

Nicky Jefferies (Skin Deep) *is in the beauty business, and her holistic approach and care are amazing . . .*

'I believe that just as the 80s and 90s have been decades for the "body", so this new century will be the time of the "mind and spirit". Relaxation centres will hit new highs, as meditation, relaxation and "being" come more to the fore. The cure, care and creation of our own "selves" will be at the heart of everything we do, as we start to move towards beauty from within. When this happens, we will truly become human beings, and we will discover new ener-gies, confidence and purpose.'

Lex McKee on meditation:

'I agree totally with David on this – it is unintelligent to say that there is only one way to meditate – one position, one form. Furthermore, whilst it seeks a place of calm, quiet serenity, it is not devoid of connectivity to the existing world. If anything, it enhances one's sense of being connected.'

Perhaps this is why many of us feel disconnected when we do not take time out to pause and reflect? Choose a method and a context that has meaning for you. In my own research into the use of music to transform mental state, I have encountered experts who assert that classical music is best, sitar music is better, and rock music is destructive. The key is what the music MEANS to you. I used Led Zeppelin to prepare for my biology exams. Twenty-four years later, I can still recall some of the key content and visualise the diagrams when I hear certain tracks from Led Zeppelin III.

This shouldn't happen! So what did happen? As I reviewed my learning, the music was at an appropriate volume for me, in the background. My mind wove the music into the tapestry of my learning experience so that Led Zeppelin means Bowman's Capsules in the kidneys just as Beanz Meanz Heinz! To move you forward, I would suggest you sketch out all the things that mean calm, quiet, focus for you. Which pieces of music or sounds? Which physical position? Which colour? Which clothes? What temperature? What level of lighting? Movement or stillness? Eyes open or closed? You are the expert – you will find your own way.

If you wish to stay on Self, go to **The Fastest Way to Make Any Change in Your Life** 30 (p195)
or
If you wish to change journey, join **Leadership of People**, go to **Doom or Disaster, Welcome to Neg-Land** 20 (p129)

the fastest way to
make any change in your life

You have come from either

29 – 'The Power of State – Everyone Needs a Place to Be' (Leadership of Self)
or
20 – 'Doom or Disaster, Welcome to Neg-Land' (Leadership of People)
You are on Leadership of Self – 4 of 7

We are human beings, not human doings. We will know at any moment of our lives whether we are 'being' or whether we are 'doing' by how we feel. The most natural feeling in the world is total and absolute one-ness. Inner peace.

Too often we live our lives in reverse. 'If I get promoted then I will do my job better because I will have value and then I will BE a better leader.' Or, 'if I get the big job, car and house, I can drive around looking important, entertain lavishly, then I really will be somebody.'

Absolute calm is restored into our lives when we decide to live our lives in the grandest version of our grandest vision. This does not mean we walk around with a 'holier than thou', arrogant expression, quite the reverse. It is the difference between knowing, and telling, it is the difference between self, and ego. Absolute calm comes from within, and when we move from Get–Do–Be to Be–Do–Get.

How can we do this? How long will it take us? One single heartbeat. In the moment we take in, embrace and make happen, the following, life-transforming statement:

The single most powerful way to make any change in your life, is to act as if that change has already been made.

WOW!!! When I first heard this my head went into a spin – what???

Whenever I share this with others it is greeted with silence, and this always prompts my three thirds theory, as it will right now:

A third of people reading this, will believe it straight away and want to get on with it, NOW!

A third of people will be unconvinced, but interested enough to be convinced.

A third of people will be in a state of disbelief, and will never have read anything so crazy in their life, and will now have me firmly categorised as a 'wacko'.

Which of these categories do you come into? And which one of these groups is 'right'?

They all are, of course!

There is no right or wrong, there is only what serves you, and what does not. And these are simply words on a page inside a book with a strange x-ray image of a suit on the cover.

This acting 'as-if' is the complete opposite of everything I ever previously learned about success. By the way, it has many other names. If I was out to really impress you I would tell you what psychologists call it, oh, all right then – wait for it – 'autogenic conditioning'. Just a small wow this time. It's also known as 'fake it till you make it'.

But that is all irrelevant to the possibilities it opens up in our lives, and the fact that our lives can be transformed so fast. I have seen a father reconnect with his daughter, just by thinking 'as-if' – they had not been close for many years, she was at university and he was working every hour there was.

He wanted to re-ignite their relationship, their friendship, and their love. And so he wrote his outcome:

'I will have a close, loving relationship with Rebecca, based on mutual trust, openness and friendship.'

I asked him to word it in the present, in the 'as-if'. He said OK and wrote:

'I will have a close, loving relationship with Rebecca, based on mutual trust, openness and friendship.'

His brain would not allow him to do it – after all, we all

know that success is something that happens in the future, it cannot happen NOW. Success is something we all aspire to, it cannot be here, with us. NOW. After all, it takes time to achieve, often many years of grind and hardship, it cannot arrive NOW.

It can, and it does, and it did for my friend. I took a pen, and crossed out just one word.

'I ~~will~~ have a close, loving relationship with Rebecca, based on mutual trust, openness and friendship.'

And his life changed forever. One pen stroke made in one heartbeat. He looked at the piece of paper and left the room, mobile phone in hand. I knew who he was going to call... and that was four years ago, and I am delighted, humbled, to report that father and daughter are doing well, and two people could not be closer.

Let us look at what happened here: from 'I will have a close, loving relationship with Rebecca, based on mutual trust, openness and friendship'; to 'I have a close, loving relationship with Rebecca, based on mutual trust, openness and friendship.'

Any judgement of 'right' or 'wrong' was bypassed and a new reality born. Put quite simply, as human beings:

We automatically move in the direction of our most dominant thoughts.

What we think about, we are. This new sentence transformed his thinking, his relationship, and his life. It was his new reality, and when we believe something to be true, we see the world in that way.

We have a conscious mind, and a subconscious mind, but that really doesn't matter – because by using 'as-if' we harmonise everything.

THE NAKED LEADER

And he took immediate action – NOW – after all, as he has such a relationship, NOW, he will act in a certain way.

I have had the privilege to work with over a thousand leaders (i.e. people) throughout the world. Among these are hundreds of amazing stories, including:

- **The woman who announced on day one that she had the worst memory in the world, and after 'as-if' she had the best memory (and is now a memory champion).**

- **The team who had never been as one – they had always argued, been in dispute and had no respect for each other. A weeklong team-building event did not help, either. And then they all decided to act 'as-if' they were one team. And guess what?**

And my personal favourite:

- **The nephew of a very close friend of mine, a boy of nine who was very unhappy, and no one could reach the root cause. When he came to visit us once, I asked him if he would like to play a game – called the 'happy game' – in which we both had to act 'as-if' we were very happy (deliriously so, on this occasion). We told each other jokes and quickly reached the stage of laughing just for the sake of it. After we finished, he was in a far better 'state' than when we started – because it is simply not possible to act happy without actually *being* happy.**

When we do 'as-if' in our lives, we move from Get–Do–Be to Be–Do–Get. And if any of you are saying, 'What about when reality catches up?' you will come to that later in your journey.

There is one other, very powerful element to all of this. In our lives, there are three aspects that determine if we can achieve something, be successful, and be more than what we have become. These are:

- **Our experience;**
- **Our knowledge; and**
- **Our imagination.**

Which plays the biggest part? Funnily enough, if you ask people with more experience, they say experience, and if you ask people with 'knowledge' (say, newly qualified students) they say 'knowledge'.

Actually, while these are both important, it is our imagination that plays the biggest single part in our achievements, our leadership and our lives, by far.

If you doubt the power of our imaginations, go and see a horror film. You know the story is not real, that they are actors wearing masks, so why are you clinging onto the person next to you (very embarrassing if you do not know them!). Or . . . read a book, or watch TV, or have a dream, or . . .

The reason our imaginations are so powerful is because our minds cannot tell the difference between something that happens in 'reality' and something we imagine with emotional intensity. Psychologists have known this for years, and yet it is only recently that we have realised the full impact this can have.

It opens up the realities of guided visualisations (taking people into their ideal future, in their minds, guiding them to work out how they got there, and bringing them back to today, armed with a complete plan for achieving the future of their dreams). It allows us to explore this thing we call reality in totally new ways, and most importantly it allows us to act 'as-if'.

I love guided visualisations, because they are so powerful. Most people think they are at the cutting edge of leadership – not bad for something that is hundreds of years old! And one of the most powerful applications, combined with 'as-if' is golf.

If you have ever hit a perfect golf shot, then you are capable of doing that any time that you wish, you simply have to be in exactly the same state as you were.

Now, imagine you have a handicap of 12, and want a handicap of 9. By applying 'as-if' you will write, take in and believe at a very deep level, not:

I will have a handicap of 9;

but rather:

I have a handicap of 9.

And presto, you now have that. Don't believe me? (You are not a cynic, and I am not batty, you are just in a different 'third' from me!) Remember:

- *We automatically move in the direction of our most dominant thoughts;*

- *When we believe something to be true, we see the world in that way; and*

- *Our minds cannot tell the difference between something that happens in 'reality' and something we imagine with emotional intensity.*

Now, here is the critical part – next time you go out and play, say you hit a 12.

What happens next will decide your future golf handicap. You can either, like most people, throw your clubs down, use some choice words, rush home and tear up this book and go back to being a 12, or . . . say to yourself, 'That's strange, I have a 9 handicap, why would I hit a 12?' You must tell yourself this with absolute conviction, closing off all other possibilities. You are a 9 and you hit a 12. Oh well, next time.

And, whichever you believe, is your choice, and no one else's.

Of course you will practise (golf) regardless of which option applies to you. But I absolutely guarantee you that those in the second category will reach 9 before those in the first, because our imaginations are so very, very powerful . . . and if you still don't believe me, here is a true story . . .

Major James Nesmeth had a dream of improving his golf game – and he developed a unique method of achieving his goal. Until he devised this method, he was just your average weekend golfer, shooting in mid-to-low nineties. Then, for seven years, he completely quit the game. Never touched a club. Never set foot on a fairway.

Ironically, it was during this seven-year break from the game that Major Nesmeth came up with his amazingly effective technique for improving his game – a technique we can all learn from. In fact, the first time he set foot on a golf course after his hiatus from the game, he shot an astonishing 74!

He had cut 20 strokes off his average without having swung a golf club in seven years! Unbelievable. Not only that, but his physical condition had actually deteriorated during those seven years. What was Major Nesmeth's secret? Visualisation.

You see, Major Nesmeth had spent those seven years as a prisoner of war in North Vietnam. During those seven years, he was imprisoned in a cage that was approximately four and one-half feet high and five feet long. During almost the entire time he was imprisoned, he saw no one, talked to no one and experienced no physical activity. During the first few months he did virtually nothing but hope and pray for his release. Then he realised he had to find some way to occupy his mind or he would lose his sanity and probably his life. That's when he learned to visualise. In his mind, he selected his favourite golf course and started playing golf.

Every day, he played a full 18 holes at the imaginary country club of his dreams. He experienced everything to the last detail. He saw himself dressed in golfing clothes. He smelled the fragrance of the trees and the freshly trimmed grass. He experienced different weather conditions – windy spring days, overcast winter days, and sunny summer mornings. In his imagination, every detail of the tee, the individual blades of grass, the trees, the singing birds, the scampering squirrels and the lay of the course became totally real. He felt the grip of the club in his hands. He instructed himself as he practised smoothing out his down-swing and the follow-through on his shot.

Then he watched the ball arc down the exact centre of the fairway, bounce a couple of times and roll to the exact spot he had selected, all in his mind. In the real world, he was in no hurry. He had no place to go. So in his mind he took every step on his way to the ball, just as if he were physically on the course. It took him just as long in

*imaginary time to play 18 holes as it would have taken in
reality. Not a detail was omitted.*

*Not once did he ever miss a shot, never a hook or a
slice, never a missed putt. Seven days a week. Four hours
a day. Eighteen holes. Seven years. Twenty strokes off. Shot
a 74.*

If you wish to stay on Leadership of Self go to **The Most
Powerful Questions on Earth... Plus...** 47 (p299)
If you wish to change journey, join **Leadership of
Company**, go to 'Oh, I've Had Such a Curious Dream!'
25 (p161)

THE NAKED LEADER

leadership by magazine

You have come from either:

9 – 'Who's to Blame?' (Leadership of Culture)
or
– 'Influence in Company Meetings'
14 (Leadership of Skills)
You are on Leadership of Culture – 6 of 7

Many leaders tell me that one of their biggest gripes is 'management by magazine'. An internal envelope arrives from the chief executive, or finance director, with a cutting/article from a newspaper/management journal. Scrawled across the top are words like: 'What are we doing on this?' or, worse still, 'Just bringing this to your attention.' E-mails with the same message, copied to the top power players in the organisation, are even more infuriating.

As if you are unaware of the big issues, or don't already have enough to read. Also, too many of these 'helpful' communications are only made for political gain – the 'Look at me, aren't I clever?' syndrome.

Such approaches must be treated carefully, and with far more respect than they deserve. Reacting negatively causes problems in itself, and puts you on the defensive, while a polite thank-you, saying this is already in hand, may commit you and your resources to a low priority area.

It is time for leadership by magazine – a third route, which has the additional benefit of reversing the pressure and putting you at the heart of your company's thinking. It is also a genuine way of drawing your board's attention to the need for investment in your area.

Start sending cuttings/e-mails and Web downloads to your CEO and other directors. Make them more paranoid than they already are – about your competitors and what they are up to, about the new, young and hungry competition that is emerging all the time, and about the need to make fast decisions and take decisive action, to drive your company forward.

There are three levels you can take, depending on the response you desire:

● **Send a relevant clipping about a competitor in the internal mail. Write on it, 'Thought you would find this of interest, we can easily do better – let's discuss ASAP.'**

● **Send an e-mail to the CEO/FD copying the whole board. Highlight a new company that will be a threat to you, and** add one paragraph about how you can utilise the inherent resources you already have to 'squash them before they get started'.

- Send a private e-mail just to your CEO, saying, 'There are industry developments which represent a serious and direct threat to the future of the organisation. These are so urgent they require face-to-face discussion and speedy action. Please call me at your earliest opportunity.' On this one, you will need to have a clear understanding of the new, and existing threats that are out there, with clear plans for how to overcome them.

Your approach will largely depend on your relationships and existing influence. If you are already at the centre of board level decisions, you will not have to pursue this route. However many leaders are not taken seriously by their organisations at the highest levels. This route of action will ensure the door to the CEO opens. It will then be up to you to walk through, and make sure it never closes again.

I put this into practice many times with directors I work with. One was complaining that his CEO never called him, and he felt ignored and undervalued. He wanted just ten minutes with his boss, could I help him? Absolutely. I had him send the following e-mail, similar to the one above:

(Names changed!)

Heading – 'Private and Urgent' (Two of the most magnetic words in any language)

Dear Graham,

There is an article in today's Financial Times *that repre-sents a serious and direct threat to the future of the organisation. This is so urgent it requires face-to-face discussion and speedy action.*

Please call me as soon as you receive this.

With best wishes,

Alistair
Ext. 467

Four minutes later – that's FOUR MINUTES – Graham called: could Alistair see him right now?

Alistair turned to me. 'Thank you, what do I do now?'
I reached for the FT, 'Now we find the article'.

If you wish to stay on Leadership of Culture, go to **Room 101** 19 (p125)
or
If you wish to change journey, join **Leadership of Skills**, go to **Building Total and Absolute Rapport** 41 (p257)

THE NAKED LEADER

values-based leadership

You have come from either:

21 – 'Following the Lines and Breaking the Rules' (Leadership of Culture) – 4

or

36 – 'Inspiration Just Got Real' (Leadership of People) You are on Leadership of Culture – 2 of 7

There is a way to break out of the boom-or-bust cycle, to ensure your people, team and organisation thrive during good times and bad, and it has nothing to do with process, product or projects.

It has everything to do with perception, people and passion. People will only ever 'buy' into an idea if they believe in it, or, more importantly, if they believe in you.

Everyone hates to be sold to, but they love to buy into an idea, an initiative or innovation. They must feel they have that choice, and they must feel involved. Both of these are simple to achieve, so why haven't more organisations done this?

Firstly because of the egos of the senior managers, let's call them the ego-suits. Their egos tell them that their power comes from their position, from attending meetings that others are not invited to (often off-site and very hush-hush, sadly often in a crummy hotel), and these egos tell them to keep almost everything to themselves. The fact that very little in an organisation needs to be kept secret (other than personal and competitor information) is of no consequence to the ego-suits.

It's not their 'fault', of course, they have worked hard to reach this position. True, they did promise that things would be different when they got there, more open, more involvement, more democracy, but hey, times change.

And so they walk around with knowing looks, clutching important-looking papers close to their chest paranoid more about whether what is being proposed is being kept secret, rather than if it will actually work.

Do you really want to go through everything we went through before?

Placing value, and values, at the heart of our organisation, is important for so many other reasons, beyond people, culture and leadership. Most companies are realising the importance of corporate and ethical responsibility to their customers, their stakeholders, society and to each other. Integrity and trust have taken on a new significance, following years of deception and deceit that hid behind the veil of such meaningless words as 'quality' and 're-engineering'. People will simply not want to work for unethical companies, customers will shop elsewhere, and legal disputes will always be a risk. Ethics and success just became powerful partners.

Many people call this 'Corporate and Social Responsibility'. I call it 'Personal Responsibility'.

There are three levels of values that lie at the centre, the very centre of a true, 21st-century company.

I offer these values merely as guidance, and the three for each of you as leader, your team and your organisation cover general approaches, behaviours and culture. Please, put in place your own words that mean something for you.

Place your values at the heart of everything you do, say and are, and you will transform your lives.

The values I offer for you as a leader are:

- **Contribution**: Giving first, putting others first, helping first, seeing the world through others' eyes. Have the ethos that you are here to serve others, and you will not just earn a living, you will live a life.

- **Integrity**: Being as one in everything you do, everything you say and everything you are. You trust everyone 100% when you meet them, expecting them to meet that trust. You are honest in everything you do, honest to yourself and others.

- **Enlightenment:** You live each and every day in the grandest version of your grandest vision, are always looking to learn from others, and help others. You believe in the fundamental good in people and in the human spirit.

For your team:

- **Openness**: Behind closed doors you are open with each other. That means you trust each other, and share the truth without fear or favour. This is not easy as we do not want to hear negative things about ourselves, especially from our peers. However, openness need not be negative, but it has to happen. Only when you know the truth, the real issues in your team, can you move forward.

- **Togetherness**: Inside the team, debate, discuss and decide – then go forward with one voice. Providing everyone has had a chance to have a say, and been genuinely listened to, they will go forward with you. 'One team – One vision'.

  This does not mean you are 'against' other teams (we can all be in more than one team), it does mean that we unite behind a common purpose. And we never, ever run down another member of our team, except in private, with that person.

- **Respect**: We all have unique strengths, and we respect each other's skills and talent. You do not need to like each other (it would be a tedious world if we all liked each other), but you do need to respect each other, and be there for each other. Unstoppable teams are like a single force of power: 'We believe in us'.

And for your organisation:

- **Passion**: How does your organisation 'feel'? – Is there a buzz, an excitement, a feeling of genuine oneness? Are people smiling, thriving in what they do, and fulfilled? Do they all know the values of the company, do they feel involved, and have you won over both their hearts and

their minds? Passion happens through cultural transformation, and nothing less.

- **Humour**: Fun. I once put this up as a proposed value and
  everyone laughed. True, they were laughing at me, but it
  was a start, they were laughing. And why shouldn't we
  enjoy our work? I am not talking about at the expense of
  other people, I am talking about keeping things in perspective, about helping each other smile, about feeling great
  about being where we are.

- **Determination**: Call it what you will – persistence,
  commitment, this is about relentless persistence to reach
  your own defined success, while doing things right. This is
  about not giving up, and more, it is about helping others get
  there as well, it is about doing what's right, it is about
  integrity on a huge scale.

The future must be different, and it can be, from this
moment on. Wherever you are reading this, on a train, at
home or on holiday, stop reading right now, and check the
time, and date. For if you so choose, your life will change
forever, right now.

OK, now resolve that you will become a 21st-century
leader, that you will lead your team and family into times
of greater success and fulfilment, and you will play a huge
part in helping your organisation leap forward to a new
tomorrow. And you will start this now.

*Ethical behaviour, responsibility to others, and an example
of personal contribution, integrity and enlightenment, from
a five-year-old boy . . .*

Picture the scene. School sports day at junior school. It's the 50-metre race for five-year-olds. There are about 20 children entered. I notice that one of the children is allowed to start further up the field than the rest – my friend tells me this is because this girl has slight learning difficulties. The race begins and there is a mad rush for the line, with parents cheering on their loved ones. Unfortunately, the start given has not helped the little girl, and she is quickly overtaken as the others race to win. Most runners complete the race, and then something happens, an amazing thing. A boy who is about to cross the line, suddenly stops. He stands there, alone, and waits for the girl who had the start, to cross the line before him, so that she would not be last. True story, my eyes filled with tears, and I was not alone.

* * *

Joe Crosbie, as a charity marketer, was becoming uncomfortable with charity marketing, which was becoming increasingly shocking and/or guilt led. The analogy he drew was people responded to charity appeals because after reading them they 'needed' to make a gift to allow themselves to return to the state they were in prior to receiving the charities message. Much the same way as a smoker needs nicotine to return to normal.

Joe's professional goal is now to create better communications that return helping behaviour to a positive choice. Specifically, after receiving the communication and making the gift the person feels better than before, thereby making supporting charities a positive, life enriching experience that is welcomed.

Joe is a leading exponent of value-based marketing, in

THE NAKED LEADER

which consumers seek a more responsible behaviour from companies.

'Today people are actively involved in boycotting goods and services for reasons not related to price or quality. They say that companies should engage in corporate social responsibility even if it means higher prices; are more likely to buy goods and services from companies that commit to social and community concerns; and think that a key differentiating factor for a company is social responsibility.

'Companies previously differentiated by "price or quality" are seeking unique characteristics to build reputations that will distinguish them from their competitors in the marketplace.

'"Values Based Marketing" emphasises the ethical conduct and community involvement as one of the most important drivers of a company's reputation.'

If you wish to stay on Leadership of Culture, go to **Recapture The Magic . . .** 23 (p147)
or
If you wish to change journey, join **Leadership of Self**, go to **Living as a Leader** 2 (p39)

modelling

You have come from either:

44 – 'The Choice of Opposites' (Leadership of Skills)
or
37 – 'One Team – One Voice' (Leadership of Teams)
You are on Leadership of Skills – 7 of 7

As business leaders, we are drowned in best practice. Armies of academics, researchers and gurus publish, present and patter on about it. But what does it mean? And does it have a role in meeting the challenges of the new business age?

To me, best practice means applying what works across a large number of organisations, in your own. With so many universal truths around (the same challenges that face every company) this approach has a role to play, but if you really want to stand out from the crowd, only a limited one.

Because the future is not what it used to be. Doing the same as everyone else is no longer enough – it is only by doing something different that you will move ahead, and it is only leaders, teams and companies that move ahead who will survive and thrive.

There is an alternative to best practice, which will enable you to soar ahead of the majority, without risk-taking; it is called modelling. Modelling means seeking out the very best, finding someone, or an organisation, that has achieved what you wish to achieve, and doing what they did.

In leadership terms we are talking about modelling excellence, seeking out those who are succeeding. It fits in perfectly with being a Naked Leader; people who are successful leave behind them clues that we can learn from.

The cynics may call this cheating, or copying, or the opposite of free thinking; nothing could be further from the truth. We all look for teachers and coaches in human and corporate excellence, we all seek to learn from the masters.

Those who do it also know that simply following the same recipe as others is not enough, it must be adapted to your own organisation's specific challenges and goals. There is still some risk, and a need for bravery. Modelling will provide the map and compass, you still have to lead the way.

The key difference between best practice and modelling is the difference between the many and the few. Those who model the very best are still moving away from the general masses – rather than doing what works in every company. Best practice is also traditionally focused on solving problems, and has developed a tired, boring, consultancy-led image. Modelling is about being where you want to be, and embarking on an exciting journey.

How do you model? Find a person, a company or a team that has achieved what you want to achieve, that is living the reality of your dreams. You can find these people through conferences, award ceremonies and simple networking. Then seek to understand how they did what they did – be open with them about your motives – modelling is the sincerest form of flattery.

Then do what they did, constantly adjusting your actions according to the results you achieve.

Modelling is the fastest, most effective and powerful way to achieve anything, and when everyone is doing it, it will become best practice. Then it is time to move on, and once again seek out another champion to model. Or, more likely, by now thinking and acting like the first exemplar you modelled, you will become a true pioneer, and a role model for others.

Whatever we want to change in our lives, there is a very good chance that someone else has achieved it before us. Often, it is the hype, mystery and jargon put in our way. Take the diet industry. It doesn't matter where you look – women and men's magazines alike, there on the cover is a thin person (always with a massive grin, and usually with the word sex somewhere nearby). We buy the magazine because we want to look like they do, and then we discover that to do this we need to follow some ridiculous eating regime, or exercises, or we have to follow 'The

Portscatho Diet'. Let me tell you a secret – huddle up – the way to lose weight is to burn off more calories than you consume. These magazines know this, of course, but they have to make it all appear complex and complicated. And it's not. So, cut out the picture that you wish to model, recycle the rest of the magazine, and make your decision, closing off all other options.

You have completed Leadership of Skills, go to
Enlightened Leadership 42 (p263)
or
If you wish to change journey, join **Leadership of Culture**, go to **Room 101** 19 (p125)

hidden account management

You have come from either:

6 – 'Job Evaluation in the Bin' (Leadership of Company)
or
17 – 'Integrity-based Networking' (Leadership of Career)
You are on Leadership of Company – 4 of 7

I used to think that the success of your team and department depended as much on what people thought of you, as on the service you provided. This caused much upset to those companies peddling 'quality' and 'balanced scorecards', who argued that what we do in reality is all.

With the publication of this book, I am happy to admit I was wrong. I now *know* that the success of your business department, team, and for you as a leader depends *totally* on what people think of you. Perception is absolutely everything – it is reality, and people have different perceptions all the time (some call this their 'maps of the world'), proving that at any one time we are surrounded by multiple realities!

Our future is now decided not by what we do, but by what people think we do, and how they believe we do it. What we actually do is almost irrelevant. There is one proviso in this – I am assuming that everyone reading this is an ambitious leader, wants to do and be their best, i.e. they do not come into work with the intent to completely sabotage their companies. Every single business team I know, and I know a fair number, works hard and long, has dedicated people, and is focused on success.

So, it comes down to perception. Focus on improving, better still, transforming perception, and you will be popular, and will become the supplier of choice in your organisation, in other words your business customers will want to use your services, rather than feel they are being forced to do so.

How can this be done – fast?

It is mission-critical to make friends in key areas of your business. This may not seem fair, but it is reality, and the key is to make reality work to your advantage.

The single most powerful way to do this, and to alter and manage perception, is through something I call 'hidden account management'. The success of this lies in how we are as human beings – how we think and feel is governed by something called association, i.e. the meaning an event has for us will depend on what we associate that event with. If you hear a piece of music on the radio that you heard on a special night out with your first love, it will immediately and automatically trigger you to feel as you did at that time.

The best illustration of this comes from the world of information technology (IT), but it can be applied across every service team in any organisation. When organisations used to make money as a matter of course, it didn't matter what IT's 'users' thought of their IT department, after all, few people could ever find them!

Then they went through a phase of hiding under their desks when a problem happened – 'The system's down' – quick, under a desk. Next, and most recently, they were told they had to become more 'customer-focused'. When anything went wrong they put on their training shoes and ran around the building and company, saying to anyone and everyone: 'We have a problem, I'm sorry'. Often whole armies would do this.

The effect of this, of course, was to associate, in the company's mind, the appearance of anyone from IT with a problem, as *the only time they would meet their internal customers was when things were going wrong.*

Ask yourself this, how many times are you and your team only seen when things are going wrong?

Hidden account management takes these principles of association, and combines with our lessons from history, to powerful advantage, by making sure that our companies consistently catch us doing something right!

Here is how it works – draw up a list of the ten or so most powerful decision makers in your company – the people in whose hands your future sits. Make sure you include personal assistants, and that guy in underwriting who has been here 25 years and holds more power than his job title suggests. Then list the top ten communicators in your department. (Numbers will depend on size of company, of course.) And now for the magic – simply match each person on the left, with one on the right, and the person on the right (in your team) has one overriding aim – to make sure the person they are 'managing' catches your team doing things right, time and time again.

This is, quite simply, the most powerful and proven way to raise perception in your company. A few words of warning, it must be kept secret (hidden), rotate your people allocated every two months, and don't use this to replace traditional account management, which still has a role. Account management focuses on areas and departments, hidden account management on people.

People, and what they think of us, are the key.

The active promotion of your team's services, and results, is a growing priority on business leaders' agendas. This should happen both openly and behind closed doors.

This may sound manipulative – it is. However, it is for the right reasons, and with the right results for everyone. For years service departments have suffered poor perception, now we have a way not just to reverse the trend, but to see it soar. That will buy us time, and support, to carry out our roles and achieve even more.

One final comment, it works beautifully with external customers, as well. Make sure you are communicating with them when things are going well, and not just in response to complaints, and you will have true loyalty – that's not handing them meaningless discount cards, it's having them buy from you because they love you.

By the way, it is important to keep this hidden when we do this internally. Those top influencers will love being treated specifically, but they would never want to know that you were doing it deliberately. I know one director who did this openly and it backfired before it started. His boss told him to treat everyone equally.

Many organisations judge their internal people by 'service level agreements'.

Train companies have perfected these to an art second to none. They publish their graphs every month, with the underlying comment that nothing that has ever gone wrong has anything to do with them.

And so many internal service departments do the same. Why do SLAs not work? Because service of every kind is an emotional experience, not a process.

If you want to see the flaws in this approach, do the following:

Persuade your partner to cook you a very special meal. When it is ready sit down and start eating it. Say nothing at all, do not make any eye contact, simply eat. When you have finished, move the plate away, and look them in the eyes – then say: 'Thank you for that meal, it was satisfactory'.

And if that upsets them, reassure them by adding: 'It met my expectations'.

Then, run…

* * *

So, how are internal departments viewed by each other?

How would our colleagues have reacted if they had been on board the Titanic?

Our chief executive would not really have noticed, until his personal assistant pointed out that there was more ice in his whisky than usual. Just before the ship sank, he received his large 'golden goodbye' bonus . . .

Our finance director would make some urgent calls to the City to test investor interest, in an attempt to at the very least liquidate the company, and at most float it . . .

The HR director would run around the ship shouting that people were the most important thing on board, and now was the perfect time to put all of that empowerment training into good practice. Those courses that tell us we are empowered to do exactly what we are told to do . . .

The internal auditor would monitor closely what we were all doing wrong in trying to survive. They would not comment or intervene, safe in the knowledge that we would receive a 200 page report entitled 'could do better' in a month's time . . .

Our marketing director would spend the time making amendments to the brochure (memo to ad agency, please remove the 'un' from 'unsinkable'). As the ship was sinking, staff would be ordered to segment the deckchairs by colour . . .

Our management consultant would quickly submit an invoice, pointing out the key resources we were missing (another ship, not enough lifeboats etc.), and organise a Titanic *process re-engineering session in which we would all try to cover up the holes in the ship with post-it notes . . .*

The sales director would immediately start to promote

diving holidays, not to mention cutting an excellent deal on available lifeboats . . .

And inside IT . . .

Our IT project manager would quickly consult Prince2 and discover that the iceberg did not show up at all, and therefore must logically not be there at all . . .

Our infrastructure support team would rush around the ship shouting random times by which the ship would be 'fixed' . . .

Our help desk would still be disputing whether the SOS really was a priority-one call . . .

Our telecoms expert would find the last lifeboat available, and then announce it would take a month to launch it because of its advanced technology . . .

And finally, our wonderful IT director. Well, if he or she had been at the helm of the Titanic, the ship would have missed the iceberg completely . . . by two years.

(With thanks to Chris Yapp)

If you wish to stay on Leadership of Company, go to
Leadership by E-Mail 51 (p333)
or
If you wish to change journey, join **Leadership of Skills**,
go to **Awesome Presentations** 48 (p307)

making success so easy to achieve, and failure impossible

You have come from either:

15 – 'Your Team – From Good to Unstoppable' (Leadership of Teams)

or

23 – 'Recapture The Magic . . .' (Leadership of Culture)
You are on Leadership of Teams – 3 of 7

Why is it, in our lives, that we make success so hard to achieve, and failure so easy? Because of our definitions of success, and failure, and because of our 'rules' (or beliefs, or truths) about them, as they apply to our lives. It simply does not have to be this way.

The table below is exactly how we as human beings

think, every day. It is a faithful reproduction of any one of over a hundred workshops I have carried out on accelerated leadership and success – these are real parents saying these . . .

Question: What do you have to do to be a success/failure as a parent?

Success	Failure
Give them love	Raise my voice
and	or
Time	Condemn their music as 'noise'
and	or
Set an example	Go on about how lucky they are
and	or
Never talk down to them	Forgetting the name of any of their friends
and	or
Ensure their safety	Keeping them waiting for more than 30 seconds when I am collecting them
and	or
Always understand them	Not going to bed on time
and	or
Help them with homework	Hearing me swear
and	or
Teach them respect	Their being unhappy
and hundreds of others . . .	and hundreds of others . . .

I have missed off some of the more bizarre contributions

such as – for success – 'feed them', and – for failure – 'drop them in a pond' . . .

I am sure you see the difference between the two columns. When I share this at an event, few see it straight away – I certainly did not when it was first presented to me.

The left hand column has 'and', the right hand column, 'or'. Simple, and yet how each person on this planet thinks. Each and every day, we give ourselves this impossible list, for our days to be successful:

'I must have slept well, and the bathroom must be clear, and breakfast must be ready and the road must be free and the train must be empty and no one better be talking on a mobile phone . . .' and then it's still only 9 a.m.!

However, one thing happens that goes 'wrong' and we label ourselves a failure. We raise our voice at our partner, we send off an aggressive e-mail, we miss the train . . . and we have such a go at ourselves, saying, in effect, 'Why am I such a bad . . . useless . . . terrible . . . idiot?' And of course, the evidence comes flooding back to tell us . . .

Oh dear, a downward spiral that happens every day, that many people call 'life'.

And yet it doesn't have to be this way. We can change this very quickly, powerfully and in a way that will change our lives forever. How?

We switch the 'and' and the 'or'.

And we can do this, in our minds, at anytime that we choose.

So . . .

Success	Failure
Give them love	Raise my voice
or	and
Time	Condemn their music as 'noise'
or	and
Set an example	Go on about how lucky they are
or	and
Never talk down to them	Forgetting the name of any of their friends
or	and
Ensure their safety	Keeping them waiting for more than 30 seconds when I am collecting them
or	and
Always understand them	Not going to bed on time
or	and
Help them with homework	Hearing me swear
or	and
Teach them respect	Their being unhappy
and hundreds of others . . .	and hundreds of others . . .

Question – Which table gives us a greater chance of success?

Question – Which table makes failure almost impossible to achieve?

The answer is obvious.

Now, many of you will be thinking the very question that I always get at events:

'Yes, David, I see that, but doesn't this mean we are lowering our standards of success, I thought your message was reach high and be all that you want to be?'

Absolutely not lowering standards, absolutely reach higher. This is a success-critical point. By rewarding yourself on an ongoing basis, by recognising that each and every behaviour in the left hand column is a success in itself, you will actually go on and achieve far more than you ever thought possible. Launch clichés – 'Nothing succeeds like success' and 'Success breeds success' – absolutely, every time.

If you raise your voice to your child does that make you a failure as a parent? No, absolutely not, it makes you a human being. And if your teenage son says he loves you, for the first time in years, is that a success? Absolutely – open the champagne, he may not say it again for some time.

In itself this is life-changing, when combined with changing definitions it becomes world changing.

Success and failure – what definitions for these 'badges of life' serve you, and what do not? The most powerful definition I have ever found is to give success a very clear definition, and failure a definition that gives us back control . . .

How about . . . Success is personal to you, and it is whatever you want it to be... it has a very specific definition and you will know when you have achieved it . . . and . . . Failure means giving up.

Failure is neither 'good' nor 'bad', and by defining it in this way, you take command of it and ownership of your life. You can still choose to give up if you wish . . . or you can choose, decide, for the really important things in your life, simply never to give up. And if you do this, you will never, ever fail.

One final thing, are your past 'failures' in your mind, or are they where they belong, in a library?

I used to have a hectic 'each day must deliver' list, proba-bly a list in my mind about 300+ long. By the end of the day I was exhausted . . . and then I changed my 'rules'. My rule for happiness now is simple – 'I am happy when I am above ground and breathing'. It serves me well, and I am a lot happier than I used to be. And, no, don't ask how I cope on the Underground . . .

If you wish to stay on Leadership of Teams, go to **Project Leadership** 43 (p273)
or
If you wish to change journey, join **Leadership of Self**, go to **Synchronicity** 8 (p71)

THE NAKED LEADER

inspiration just got real

You have come from either:

49 – 'Leadership in Times of War...' (Leadership of People)

or

43 – 'Project Leadership' (Leadership of Team)
You are on Leadership of People – 3 of 7

I believe that our lives are shaped by certain, critical moments. It is in those moments that we make a decision, a true decision, closing off all other options. We decide that events must change, and we move forward with an incredible persistence.

One of these was when we learned to walk. Much can

be learned about life, leadership and achievement through this experience. Indeed, every single thing that we do in our lives involves exactly the same process.

Picture the scene, and events, of a child learning to walk.

As a father, or mother, or relation, or parent-to-be (I am trying to cover all the bases here) you will sit down with the child (let's give her a name, let's call her Susan, and we'll assume she is a girl), and you say something like: 'Now, pay attention Susan, you are 12 months old and it's about time you started thinking about learning to walk. Now, I've drawn up a mission statement for you, and put all of the relevant information into my spreadsheet, so here are your strategic milestones, and subject to a detailed risk analysis this project looks achievable in xxx months . . .'

Susan stares at you and giggles (a bit like your team do when you make the same speech, except they giggle on the inside).

Of course you don't do this. But have no fear. If you think this approach is callous, just wait until you hear what the human potential industry (sic) calls Susan's walking journey.

When she can't walk, and does not know she cannot walk, she is *unconsciously incompetent*! (Susan sleeps in her cot and crawls around, quite happy), and then she moves to being . . . *consciously incompetent*. She can't walk, but now knows that walking is a different way of getting around. She notices other people getting around on two legs while she is on 'four'. (Susan crawls around, and takes her first trial steps on two legs and falls over. Huge positive response from all around her, as long as she is unhurt – the only time you can laugh at a child falling over and get away with it. Susan gets up, encouraged by the warmth and shouts in the room), and then she moves to being . . . *consciously competent*. She can now walk, but has to focus on it, and really concentrate, until she moves to being *unconsciously competent* when she walks around.

Everyone goes through this cycle in everything they learn for the first time.

And the key point in it all, is the point at which most people give up, the point that requires determined focus and action, the point after which, once crossed, there is no return. It happens when we move from being consciously incompetent (we know we cannot do something) to being consciously competent (we can do something, but we have to concentrate hard).

And the biggest decider by far will be how much positive energy, support and encouragement there is around at that time. If her relatives had all yelled at Susan, 'You silly girl, you fell over, take a pay cut', do you think she would have walked so quickly? And yet, that is exactly what we do to each other, so often, in our families, in our teams, in our lives.

And so, moving from conscious incompetence to conscious competence; that is the point at which you either keep going, or give up, that is your choice. That is the point at which your people, when they are learning a new skill, either keep going, or give up, and that is their choice. That is the point when inspiration either becomes real, or does not.

And so it was that in 1832 young Abraham Lincoln lost his job. And the Discouragement Fraternity sneered and said unto him: 'If you're so smart, why ain't you successful?'

And Abe, intimidated, hung his head low and crawled back under yon rock from whence he came.

And so it was that later in that same year Abe ran for the Legislature of Illinois and was badly defeated. And the Discouragement Fraternity sneered and said unto him: 'If you're so smart, why ain't you successful?' And Abe, intimidated, hung his head low and crawled back under yon rock from whence he came.

And so it was that this pattern continued – tried his hand at business in 1833 and went broke; ran for speaker in 1838 and lost; was overwhelmingly defeated in a bid for nomination of Congress in 1843; rejected for appointment to the US Land Office in 1849; soundly beaten for US Senate seat in 1854; defeated for nomination for Vice-President in 1856 – and after each failure the Discouragement Fraternity, always more than happy to be of help, sneered and said unto him: 'If you're so smart, why ain't you successful?' And each time, Abe, intimidated, hung his head low and crawled back under yon rock from whence he came.

Then in 1858, after once again being defeated for the US Senate, and after once again enduring the Discouragement Fraternity sneering and saying unto him: 'If you're so smart, why ain't you successful?', a funny thing happened on the way back to yon rock from whence he came. Abe thought for a moment, scratched his head, then finally came to the conclusion that intimidators must have more fun than intimidatees. Thus concluding, he looked up at the Discouragement Fraternity and replied: 'Stick they finger up thy nose and go fly thee a kite.'

. . . And lo and behold, Abe, the ex-intimidatee, became President . . . and saved the Union. And the members of the Discouragement Fraternity – fingers in noses and kites

THE NAKED LEADER

in hand – said unto Abe: 'Bravo! We always knew you would be successful.'

... Whereupon Abe displayed a gentle smile and walked quietly away.

From Winning Through Intimidation
by Robert J. Ringer

If you wish to stay on Leadership of People, go to **Our Next Generation** 40 (p253)
or
If you wish to change journey, join **Leadership of Culture**, go to **Values-based Leadership** 32 (p209)

one team – one voice

You have come from either:

28 – 'Project Success' (Leadership of Teams)
or

12 – 'Charisma in a Heartbeat' (Leadership of Skills)
You are on Leadership of Teams – 6 of 7

One of the biggest problems faced by our teams is the washing of dirty linen in public. One person will openly criticise the latest strategy decision, another will tell their business colleague, 'privately', that the latest initiative to improve service is 'a waste of time'. Or, after the difficult decision is made to go with a particular product, groups of people loyal to, and trained in, the unsuccessful alternative will declare civil war.

Such are the reasons behind our departments becoming disparate groups working in different directions. Within this environment it is impossible to implement lasting change, strategy and direction. Disunity is a key driver for inaction and distraction.

With so many choices and so much pressure facing our organisations, our people and ourselves, sometimes we feel we have to move like lightning just to stand still, and there seems to be so little time to discuss any decisions, let alone make one!

If uncertainty reigns at the leadership level, imagine how the department feels, kept in the dark as most are, often hearing key decisions on a need-to-know, or have-you-heard basis.

The greatest decision-making power lies deep within every department. People at the front line will have an opinion and view on the best way forward, and they should be heard. This can be achieved through open forums, at team meetings or through some other vehicle. However it is done, it is important that all views are expressed openly and without fear. It need not take long; several open meetings can air most views.

Once a decision is made it must be bought into by everyone in the department. Unity of purpose and direction is the most elusive yet one of the most powerful ways forward for all departments, teams and organisations.

If people are genuinely listened to, and healthy internal debates are allowed to thrive within an open, no-blame culture, they are happy to go along with whatever decision is made. It is when decisions are made in secret, or where the decision-making process is unclear, that problems arise and disharmony is the result.

Everyone needs to be valued.

Successful teams become a sort of autocratic democracy. Once a direction or policy is chosen, everyone will buy into it. Collective responsibility will put your team in a very strong position in everything you do.

Decisions must be clear, concise, compelling, and communicated, if they are to succeed. Do this, and you will secure a uniform understanding, and a strong, single voice, a collective approach to your customers.

Many managers delay taking firm actions on the future owing to different internal opinions, politics and pressure groups. This can have a devastating effect on service, costs and futures, and has to be addressed as a core requirement of even having a future, let alone shaping one. Leaders do not allow this to happen.

I was invited in by a business leader who told me he and his team were a shining example of openness with each other. I joined their meeting. At the start, my colleague announced my presence, and added: 'I have told David that we are all totally open with each other, that's right, isn't it?' – they all agreed in unison. What a shining example, I thought, it reminded me of those nodding dogs you get in the back of cars.

If you wish to stay on Leadership of Teams, go to **People Mean Business – Improve Performance By at Least 10%** 45 (p287)
or
If you wish to change journey, join **Leadership of Skills**, go to **Modelling** 33 (p217)

attracting the headhunters

You have come from either:

13 – 'Your CV Stands, or Falls, for You' (Leadership of Career)

or

'Following the Lines and Breaking the Rules'
21 (Leadership of Culture)
You are on Leadership of Career – 5 of 7

Headhunters make a disproportionate impact on the recruitment industry. More than half of available positions are now not advertised. Although we worry about this with regard to our people receiving those phone calls, we ourselves love to be contacted – it makes us feel special.

There is always demand for leaders who have the right skills to drive organisations forward to new futures.

As a result, people like you are in short supply.

Companies who value their people must ensure they put in place a retention plan that rewards well above the average in terms of both salary and influence.

If you are a leader who has the right skills, with a clear purpose, a passion and persistence, and you believe in yourself as a leader, the future is yours.

Although there will be many 'specials' in the Sunday paper career pages, the majority of positions, in particular the most lucrative, are still not advertised. So, how do you attract the right phone calls?

There are three ways to gain the attention of headhunters:

- **Reputation and Profile**: Make sure you are known in the industry for the excellent work you have done, and skills that you have. Speak at the right conferences, become involved in industry organisations, and be featured in the press. Have your CV up to date – keep it to one page.

- **Networking**: Absolutely crucial to becoming known in headhunting circles. Headhunters often rely on personal recommendation. Maximise every interpersonal exchange, and every opportunity to meet peers.

- **Approaching them first**: There is only a handful of leading headhunters in this country; they are easy to get to know. Phone them before they call you.

Successful headhunters know the importance of leadership and communication skills. The leader of the future will rely on these abilities above all others.

If you are a leader, ready to shape destinies, your phone will be rather busy. In that situation I suggest you adopt the poise of a cat. Meditate quietly, and internally, on all of your offers and options. Then, when you know what you want, pounce. Failure won't have a chance.

And of course headhunters must sometimes be avoided . . .

Two men were taking a break from the jungle heat, relaxing next to a lake, cooling their feet. Suddenly a wild looking headhunter leaped out of the undergrowth. He looked fit, he looked mean, and he looked hungry. One man jumped up and started running. The other started putting on his training shoes. The first man shouted back – 'Don't be stupid, you'll never outrun the headhunter.' The second man shouted back, 'I don't have to outrun the headhunter, I have to outrun you.'

(With thanks to Ian Jarvis)

If you wish to stay on Leadership of Career, go to
Succession Planning 26 (p167)
or
If you wish to change journey, join **Leadership of Teams**, go to **People Mean Business – Improve Performance By at Least 10%** 45 (p287)

making your strategies as one

You have come from either:

47 – 'The Structure of Guaranteed Success'
or

32 – 'Succession Planning' (Leadership of Career)
You are on Leadership of Company – 1 of 7

Consultants make a shed-load of money out of this thing called business alignment – but what does it mean, and how can it be achieved?

Alignment means ensuring that all services in an organisation are closely matched with business aims, culture and performance. Easy to talk about in theory, difficult to achieve in practice.

Most often, different strategies across a company are rarely matched to ensure the same approach, goals and vision. As a result, business plans often lack cohesion and become confused. With this situation, organisations do not have one direction, and no matter how fast these companies make decisions and take actions, they will go nowhere.

The most effective method of achieving total balance, a one-world vision, is to wrap each and every departmental strategy around that of the organisation as a whole, and vice-versa:

- **The board-level, corporate strategy will be put in place, with full involvement from leaders in the organisation (hopefully!).**

- **Each department's strategy will then be developed to reflect this business vision in some areas, and to drive it forward in others.**

All plans will then be mapped onto each other, section by section.

The final document will be a combination of where the organisation is going (the high level direction), and then specifically how it will be achieved. Each company goal, project and activity will be followed by how each team will help achieve it. Equally, each and every departmental project will be followed by a section providing the clear business aims, resources and benefits.

This is powerful; apart from giving a cohesive view, it helps prevent duplication of effort and resources, encourages everyone to help each other, and gives each team a view and feeling of corporate impact – tying in everyone's role to the bigger picture. This is hugely motivating for people and teams at every level.

Organisations that have mastered this approach achieve stunning improvements in driving their business forward. In addition to improved planning and understanding by all involved in the vision and journey, such contentious issues as ownership, prioritisation and delivery can be more fully explored, and explained.

The approach can be extended to other activities within an organisation, such as budget planning, training and recruitment. As it develops, the areas previously known as 'marketing', 'finance' and whatever, will begin to merge as one with the term 'business', with leaders throughout having a wider understanding of the big picture, and how it will be achieved.

Adopting this method also leads to improved measurement of your value. It will only be possible to list each and every activity as it is matched to a business justification, rather than being done for its own sake.

When reasons for spend are explained in such hard commercial language, the perception in, and influence of, every department will rise. Budget negotiations will also become easier, as they begin to take place in business language.

Everyone talks about departments being core to business activities, but it is all too rare in reality. By adopting this approach, and involving a wide range of leaders in its development and operation, the organisation will truly go forward with one vision, one voice, and as an awesome force of strategic power.

There is a conspiracy in organisations that we can only belong to one team . . . think about it as you read this true story.

The girl had been looking forward to the new kitten arriving, she had been very excited. However, now, on the very evening before it was being collected, she was very upset. Her daddy asked her why, and this is what she said:

'Well, I only have 100% of love, and I love mummy 50%, you 40% (!), my brother 2%, and the rest of my love is all taken up with the gerbils, hamsters and rabbit. I have no love left for the kitten.'

Needless to say, her daddy offered a different definition of love and she was happy again. However, how many people in your team have this 100% approach – I am in this team therefore I cannot be in any other?

If you wish to stay on Leadership of Company, go to **Organisational De-Structures** 18 (p121)
or
If you wish to change journey, join **Leadership of Career**, go to **Integrity-based Networking** 17 (p115)

our next generation

You have come from either:

36 – 'Inspiration Just Got Real' (Leadership of People)
or
5 – 'The Power of Mentoring' (Leadership of Career)
You are on Leadership of People – 4 of 7

The marketing, media and PR world seem to have grasped the concept. Most companies, regardless of size, have not.

The new business, information and knowledge experts are the young.

Game companies employ them, parents learn from them, and business pages are full of entrepreneurial stories about them. Traditional business must move fast to catch up, especially when ideas, innovation and awakening imaginations are all key to future success and achievement.

The irony is that this new opportunity-aware generation do not consider themselves geniuses, they have simply opened their minds a bit wider, and embraced the possibilities. Indeed, the very word failure does not enter their minds (until adults put it there!). And there's the rub, while we rush around focusing on everything that can go wrong, this new breed do not even think about it. And what we focus on, we become.

Combine this thought with the apparent national hunt for, and shortage of, non-executive directors, and a winning formula emerges.

Take on one of these youngsters as a non-executive director, a boardroom adviser with a two-fold brief.

- **To add their thoughts and expertise; and**
- **To widen thinking to real 'blue-sky'.**

This idea will not be popular with all. Some larger companies are so driven by complex hierarchies, politics and corporate dust they would not know how to cope with, let alone implement, such a suggestion.

Some existing managers may well find the idea unpalatable, struggling as they are to find a boardroom voice of their own.

To these people I say this. Who are the new entrepreneurs? Who are the people taking ideas and turning them into reality – fast? If they can do it on their own, just imagine what they can do for your organisation if given finance, and a free hand.

Forget the traditional business thinking, the future is not

what it used to be. You can take the lead, by finding and recommending the right person to come in at this level. What today's young may lack in business savvy they more than make up for in youthful vigour and an extraordinary capacity to learn, investigate and energise.

Where do we find such people? Through the Internet, of course. Through business schools and universities, or in one of the many net-based magazines. Just imagine, a small box advert could save you a fortune looking for that elusive non-executive director.

Consider the skills you are looking for in a non-exec. Seeing the future before it happens is likely to rank very high, as is grooming an independent, fresh point of view.

The future of successful enterprise is all about free spirits, about transforming technology, people and communications into opportunities, speed and action.

No longer can wisdom be attributed simply on the basis of age, or experience. These are important attributes and must be valued, but companies that are serious about shaping a compelling destiny will also seek out the young.

There is another, very important story about our next generation. I fundamentally believe that all children are born with equal potential. That is their birthright, and everyone is born with unique gifts, skills and talent. However, being born with equal potential does not mean being born into equal circumstances. One third of children in the UK, that's ONE THIRD, are born into poverty through no fault of their own.

The Children's Society is one of the most innovative children's charities in the country and they are not afraid to tackle some of the more difficult problems our society faces. Every year, they help more than 40,000 children and young people when they are at their most vulnerable. Their work covers a wide range of issues as they help children and young people. They believe that every child deserves a decent chance in life and, sadly, not all children get the start that they so desperately need.

Many of the one third of children born into poverty end up being disruptive at school to attract attention to the abuse or neglect they receive at home. Teachers are often overworked and under-qualified to deal with such situations and so these 'problem' children are excluded from school. They are forced to spend their days at home, often being subjected to further abuse and neglect, and life on the streets gradually seems the better option. In order to survive, stealing, prostitution and drugs become a way of life and prison is just a step away. Prison itself often makes the situation even worse.

The Children's Society aims to BREAK this cycle of deprivation as early as possible through more than 100 projects across the country covering help in the community, in schools, on the streets and to young people in prison.

If you wish to stay on Leadership of People, go to **Leaders Are Born and Not Made!** 10 (p81)
or
If you wish to change journey, join **Leadership of Career**, go to **Succession Planning** 26 (p167)

THE NAKED LEADER

building total and absolute rapport

You have come from either:

24 – 'Skills of Leadership over Management' (Leadership of Skills)

or

31 – 'Leadership by Magazine' (Leadership of Culture)
You are on Leadership of Skills – 2 of 7

What a claim; how to build total and absolute rapport with any other human being. It may be your boss, your teenage son or daughter, or someone you are meeting for the first time. Having researched this area, often called 'influence', for four years, and waded through mountains of hype, definitive 'how to' books and tapes, here it is . . . and it's dynamite . . .

Health warning: this is so powerful, it will always work, do not use it to manipulate another human being against their will.

This is the ultimate influencing technique . . .

There are three stages; they will appear very mechanical, so please interpret them according to your situation. If you are using this with someone you do not know well, follow it to the letter. If, on the other hand, you are using it with your spouse of 26 years, adapt it to the relationship you have . . .

Stage One: The other person is talking. Pay absolute attention to the other person. That means listening, not just hearing. This by itself is the biggest compliment we can pay another human being, valuing what they have to say. Listen to their words and, more importantly, be aware of their body language and movement. And all the time, you are seeking the answer to just one question . . .

Before we come to that, what will the other person talk about? They will talk about their favourite subject in the whole world, namely . . . themselves. To be more exact, they will talk about whatever subject you are discussing, from their own point of view – in the reality that they see that event or issue. By the way, they have to do this, they have no choice, they are not able to speak about any subject as if they were someone else, because it would be impossible.

And on this point, whenever anyone makes any comment about you, or expresses any opinion on you, they are merely expressing their opinion of you – and not how you actually are. This is a critical point – people can only ever express their thoughts on you, and these may depend more on how they are feeling in themselves, than on how they really feel about you. When anyone else expresses their opinion about you, in any way, it is entirely up to you – your choice – whether you accept these thoughts, or not.

So, they are talking, you are paying 100% attention, nodding and showing positive, open body language, still thinking all the time about that one question . . .

Before we come to that . . .

Stage Two: The other person is not talking, or stops. Now, what to do? Well, as human beings we only have a choice of three things we can say – we can make a statement (most often what happens during a pause), we can give a command, or we can play the most powerful card we have, and ask a question. Questions are amazing; they progress the conversation in a non-threatening way, they allow the other person to continue talking about their favourite subject, they move the discussion forward, and they focus it on a subject.

Now, you will have read books about making sure you ask open questions (any question that cannot be answered 'yes' or 'no' or with any other one-word answer), and there is a lot of human potential and influence jargon around 'precision' questions. Forget all of that, your aim here is not to worry about what label your question has, your aim is to get that person talking, so you can move forward, forward to enabling you to discover that one final, all important, finding . . .

Before we come to that, you will already have gained a deep understanding and rapport, because people love to talk about themselves and the world as they see it. Absolutely love it, and here you are, showing an interest –

becoming their new best friend.

And at every stage, with all of your energy, brainpower and powers of deduction, you are seeking the answer to the ultimate question of rapport. And here it is . . .

What is this person's most important need, right now?

I say 'need' deliberately – it's really a 'want', but it is a massive yearning need to this person.

Ideally, you will also assess one or two other 'needs' at the same time. And then, you reach over the table (metaphorically now!) pick the person up and place them in your pocket, by doing stage three:

Stage Three: You offer to help them achieve their greatest need.

Simple! Rapport built, they are nicely in your pocket . . .

Four additional points here:

1. The reason this works is because of something we all have as human beings – reciprocity. Sorry for the jargon. As human beings we have this in-built support mechanism called 'reciprocity' – if someone does something to help us we automatically want to return the favour. (This works overall in life, so do not help others on this basis, i.e. only if they help you back. They will, if you are being genuine in helping them in the first place.)

2. Do not compromise your values – in other words, if helping the other person means doing something that you do not consider 'right' do not offer. This is one reason it is useful to find out a secondary 'need' as well.

③ **Follow through. Actually do it. I know of one manager who came on a Professional Power programme and then went off building rapport with anyone and everyone he could find. Then he did not carry it through.**

④ **People often ask me, yes, but how does this work when both people know this technique? (They often say this with a large, knowing grin that says – 'Gotcha Taylor, you big headed know-all!') Answer – you have the most constructive, rapport-building and warming exchange of your life.**

However . . . most people, even those who know this awesome technique, do not do it, because they don't want to sit listening to other people, they want to talk about themselves. That's why this takes discipline, and it works.

Please tailor this to each situation. If you have been with a partner for many years you may fast track this approach.

And so I also invite you to put it into powerful reality in your personal lives. Pay absolute attention next time your partner, your child or your neighbour speaks with you. Do this with people and we see them grow, we help them shine, and we grow closer.

* * *

At a recent seminar I was asked about children. A mother was telling a captive audience about her teenage daughter, and how this simply would not work with her, because she (the daughter) either didn't say anything, or didn't shut up to allow her (the mother) to ask a question!

In the first instance, not many words are actually needed, people will always talk, act and behave in conjunction with their favourite subject, themselves, and what is important to them at any one moment. However, choose your timing. Piling twenty questions on top of a teenager who is pondering the meaning of life may not be helpful right now...

Her daughter has skipped right to stage three, and announced what is most important, for her, for here, for now.

Children always do this, they get straight to the point that is most important to them. If only adults did the same – and to think that we keep telling them to grow up!

If you wish to stay on Leadership of Skills, go to
Charisma in a Heartbeat! 12 (p89)
or
If you wish to change journey, join **Leadership of Culture**, go to **Who's To Blame?** 9 (p77)

enlightened leadership

Why do parents keep asking their children what they want to be when they grow up? Because the parents are hunting for ideas! And never has the hunt had such meaning, such power, and such momentum.

The future is not what it used to be. We are right now witnessing a significant shift in global thinking that is fast becoming a global renaissance. I believe this is going to grow, reaching its peak around 2012. I have no 'evidence' whatsoever to make this statement, I simply feel it happening all around.

I hear more people asking bigger questions, I know that Mind, Body and Spirit books are growing, and growing in popularity, and I see ethics, values and integrity at last taking their place inside organisations.

Questions such as: 'Who am I?' and, 'Why am I here?' Books such as James Redfield's *The Celestine Prophecy* and Neale Donald Walsh's *Conversations With God* (thank you Neale, thank you). And in the business world the realisation that so many consultancies have been ripping us off for too many years with their process driven initiatives which have cost us dear, and experiences such as Enron, WorldCom, Andersen's, and others, are leading to a massive demand for trust and integrity. Organisations that are unethical are finished, and good riddance.

Our next generation is taking many of these issues to heart. Of course we hear the scare stories about the young (newspapers have to sell), but for every such story there are many more positive and uplifting ones.

Wherever you have come from to read this 'final' chapter, whatever else has served you in this book, or not served you, and whatever else you now do as a result, for yourself, your team or your family, or for your community or organisation, please ask yourself these three questions:

- **What are you going to do to make a difference?**
- **Who are you and why are you here?**
- **Have you ever wondered if life has a meaning?**

Only you can ask these questions, and only you can answer them . . . Because only you know how you truly feel . . . Because only you know what it is like to be you . . . Because only you know whether you live every day, in every moment, in total, natural bliss . . .

And only you know if you have rediscovered that unlimited potential you had in those first few seconds on this earth.

No one else can answer any of these questions for you, although I am sure many people around you will try.

No matter what anyone else has ever told you in the past, above anything and everything you have ever read, heard or believed, please know this. You are a unique individual with amazing gifts, talents and abilities. You have strengths that are quite literally extraordinary, and when these are unleashed the results will astound you.

It wasn't until I was 36 that I realised I could be anything I wanted. (If you are younger than that right now, please don't leave it so late – if you are older, it's never too late!) I owe so much to Anthony Robbins for looking at me in the eyes (there were three thousand others there as well), and telling me this. Thank you, Anthony for showing me that for 36 years I had not been using my mind, my mind had been using me.

And so the doors were opened, which one would I choose?

Mark Caine said this – 'The success has this over its rivals, it knows where it is going.' And so I had discovered I could be anything I wanted to be; a few years later and I had the formula for guaranteed success, now, where was I going?

Of course, success was family, success was speaking at events and having the incredible opportunity to work with so many people, but nagging at the back of my mind, each and every day, I kept wondering… Is there more? Why am I here? What is the ultimate answer to the ultimate question?

No one has ever articulated that question so well as Douglas Adams, thank you Douglas, rest in peace.

In my travels, I have met many people who are truly at peace with themselves, they live in bliss every day, they live as human beings.

We all have different lives, and we are all so similar. In a way this book has been about what we all have in common, and what makes us all different. About those universal challenges we all face, and how some people have chosen to overcome them and move on.

What is the difference, then, for people who have truly answered these three questions:

- **What are you going to do to make a difference?**
- **Who are you and why are you here?**
- **Have you ever wondered if life has a meaning?**

1 Self over ego

We human beings spend most of our lives working to recreate the unlimited potential we had in those first few seconds on this earth. And it was absolutely without limit. It does not matter what circumstances we were born into, everyone had, and still has, an awesome inner ability. To achieve this we must look to our *selves*, and trust our higher purpose, and be aware of our ego.

The ego is the part of the self that most people present

to the world. But, unfortunately, far too many people confuse who they are with their ego. Think about individuals who define their worth by their beauty or their possessions. Or those people you know you have to be 'careful' around because they get defensive and/or hurt easily. These individuals take their ego too seriously . . . These people live for the façade, and hide the truth.

When I refer to the 'self', I am referring to the 'higher self': the part of you that is connected to nature or the universe, or God, or whatever you believe in. Your soul. Your centre. The little voice in the back of your head that knows – and tells you what you need to do. Most of the time, you won't like where the little voice is telling you to go. You will compulsively want to do what immediately feels good instead. Some of you instead fall prey to compulsively doing what feels bad – as in compulsively reacting out of guilt or shame.

But, the self is not splashy or loud, or bigheaded, that is the ego. The self knows your value, the ego has to tell everyone about it. The self understands you at a deep level, the ego tells you constantly that you need more.

In brief, the self whispers while the ego SHOUTS.

2 They put others before themselves

Everyone has value, and by respecting that, and actively having time for others, helping or perhaps simply being there, we make a difference. Everyone on this earth is connected (and I am not referring to mobile phones here!).

Occasionally we have that feeling of oneness on a national scale. The death of Princess Diana, September 11th, 2001 and the death of the Queen Mother all prompted a new feeling of care for each other.

Organisations are also (at last) beginning to realise that such initiatives as business process re-engineering do not put people at their heart. They appreciate that the only way to ethically downsize is to do so with honesty and integrity.

Everyone on this planet has value and worth; it is time to respect each other more – to have more time for each other, to really care.

3 They accept the power of forgiveness

Are your bad memories on your shoulder, weighing you down, or are they in a library? If they are still with you, carry out a peace session. Find somewhere quiet, relax and be at peace. Cover yourself mentally with a purple cloak, or curtain, make it a very deep purple, large and sweeping, and let it flow all over you. Breathe, relax.

Now, allow people who you have argued with, fallen out with, hurt, or been hurt by, to enter your mind, one by one. Perhaps start with a teacher from your school. Acknowledge them as they come into your mind, and look at them for a few seconds – they are some distance away from you, it is like watching them on a cinema screen. Now, let them go, see them disappear from your mind forever, and as you do, say to yourself, out loud or simply in your head 'I choose peace over this.'

The first time I did this, I was so happy and calm, I felt I was floating around the room.

4 They saw the future before it happened

Our minds cannot tell the difference between something that happens in reality, and something we imagine with emotional intensity. This, combined with meditation, opens up unlimited possibilities. It means we can literally relax, and place ourselves in the future – say two years hence, and imagine living the perfect day, and (the trump card) we can actually relive the previous two years to see what we did to reach where we are in our minds.

This is called guided visualisation and it is the most cutting edge technique in leadership thinking. And guess what? It is thousands of years old. Do this, it may open up a future you have never thought about before.

The best way to predict the future, is to shape it.

5 Their beliefs became their truths

No event has any meaning other than the meaning we choose to give it. This is perhaps the most powerful phrase I have ever heard in my life, because it turned everything upside down. It gave me complete command over what was happening around me. It enabled me to stop and ask myself the question, which of these many realities serve me best?

When we make this shift in our consciousness, amazing things start to happen. We look for the positives in events, we notice the energies in each other, see the wonders around us in the world. It makes our life, and our future, our choice. And it has a life-transforming impact on our lives.

Two brothers are arguing, with a passion. Who is 'right'? They both are, because they both believe what they are saying. When a penalty is awarded in a football match and the crowd reacts with total emotion – half saying 'right' (or words to that effect) and the other half saying 'wrong' (or, even more likely, words to that effect!) – who is correct?

They all are.

Two people are reading this, right now, perhaps at different corners of the globe. One decides it is the biggest load of nonsense ever, the other decides there may be something in it, and to take some actions. Who is right? They both are.

When we live our lives in our highest truth, we begin to discover who we already are, to be all that we can be, and to quite literally see the world in a different way.

No event has any meaning other than the meaning we choose to give it, and that includes life. The meaning of life is the meaning we give it.

The meaning of life is the meaning you choose to give it. Once you do this, that will be life for you, every single moment of every single day.

6 They know who they are and why they are here

The most powerful way to do this is to visit a special place. Perhaps it is a beach near your home, or a forest, or a garden. Wherever it is, make it special for you. Whenever you are in this place you feel calm, and centred. Pause from life. Take a few minutes to sit in a seat, or on the ground, or just to stand still. Be completely still.

Clear your mind completely, and just be.

Now, slowly, gently, deliberately, ask yourself the question – 'Who am I and why am I here?'

And smile, and relax, the answer may not come straight away, the answer may not come for several days or weeks, but I promise you, I promise you from my heart, that the answer will come. And when it does, you will have feelings that no words on paper can express.

You will know who you are and why you are here, and when you know this, no one – that's no one – can ever take that away from you.

What is an organisation if not its people? What is the world without each other? What would the world be like, without you in it?

The answer to everything, the meaning of life, is yours to decide. And when you do, you will have found true and total happiness, inner peace, and you will have discovered heaven on earth.

7 They live, and create, heaven on earth

When we see a word like 'heaven' (or 'God'), we give an instant reaction. When we label ideas like these they invoke much emotion and feelings. Some of you will now think this whole book has been about religion and converting you to a particular way of thinking. It has not. This whole book has been about you discovering what success means for you, and helping you make it happen.

And you will know when you have achieved it. You may not always understand why you are feeling the way you do, but you will know. In that second that you connect with another in total, absolute, unconditional love, and time seems to stand still. In that minute you take out to help another human being, and in that moment when you truly feel at one with yourself, the world and everyone in it. That is heaven on earth.

What lies before you, and what lies behind you, are but blades of grass to what lies within you.

And the story that follows is now yours, because:

- **This book is about you, not me; and**
- **It is about your success, your future and your life, not mine.**

I wish you well in all that you do, I wish you everything you wish yourself, and I thank you. Do let me know how you get on...www.nakedleader.com

Please, always know:

- **What you think about, you are;**
- **Whatever you focus on, you will become; and**
- **The best way to predict the future, is to shape it.**

Go now and live every day, in the grandest version of your grandest vision

> Please return to **The Structure of Guaranteed Success** (page 19) and select a new journey, or flick through the pages and join a journey at random, or . . .
>
> Commit now, that's right now, in private, on this page, to yourself, one success you are going to achieve, or one action you are going to take, or one person you are going to build rapport with . . .

project leadership

You have come from either:

47 – 'Making Success So Easy to Achieve, and Failure Impossible' (Leadership of Teams)
or
32 – 'Leadership by E-Mail' (Leadership of Company)
You are on Leadership of Teams – 4 of 7

Of all the subjects I write about, the two that attract most feedback are projects and leadership. Aha! Maybe there's a link. Many people now believe it is leadership that has to be our number one priority, and this also applies to our success at delivering projects. If we think about it, almost everything we do is a project, a specific outcome that happens from a team working together.

When I first came into IT, or Electronic Data Processing, four out of ten IT projects failed to go in on time, failed to meet the needs of the company, or cost too much. Business and IT leaders were unanimous, this figure had to change, and it has – it is now nine out of ten, well done IT!

In fact, well done everyone, there is no such thing as an 'IT' project, everything is a business and company project.

Forget evolution, something big has to happen. Over the last 20 years I have had the good fortune to work across a wide range of companies and projects, and I am now convinced that we need to alter our fundamental approach.

As I write this I have a marketing flyer for a project management two-day course happening next month – it is a sad document. Before I share with you my thoughts on this, please do me a favour. Close your eyes and think about someone in your team and department who delivers on projects, every time. Think about a person who you always call when the going gets tough, in the times of crisis, someone you know who will never let you down, ever.

Now think about the skills they have, the attitudes and behaviour they display consistently. I would imagine you are thinking of the following:

- **Communication;**
- **Leadership;**
- **Persistence;**
- **Inspiration;**
- **Motivation;**
- **Focus;**

- **Action, etc., etc.**

Now I glance at the document on my left, it talks about:

- **Methodologies;**
- **Planning;**
- **Spreadsheets;**
- **Bar charts;**
- **Reporting; and**
- **Project management meetings.**

There's the reason we are in the state we are in, and to me it comes down to one thing above all others – the need for project leadership, not project management.

Please don't get me wrong, the second list is important, but not as key to success as the first list. In other words, it comes down to the character, talent and person you select, over and above the traditional views on how to deliver projects. I say 'traditional' to mean what we usually think – there is nothing traditional about spreadsheets, of course, indeed, thank goodness they weren't around in ancient Egypt or we would never have got those pyramids built!

And this mismatch between what so many people think is important and what really works, continues when we recruit. Too many companies advertise for project managers with specific technical, accounting or departmental experience, who really understand processes. Instead, when recruiting for a project manager, look for three things above all else:

1. **Scars – I ask people for the biggest mistake they have ever made in a project. If they say none, it's bye-bye. The**

deeper the scars, the better.

(2) **Communication – forget the project; are they looking you directly in the eyes when they speak, are they confident, is their head high?**

(3) **Radical thinker – always remember, if they do what they have always done, they will get what they have always got. Forget 'out of the box', does the person in front of you think as if they were on a different planet? Yes? Hire them.**

No matter how much we whinge about how unfair it is to be blamed when projects fail, we always will be – it's a universal truth. We can turn that around by changing the way we run them, by appointing leaders instead of managers, and by giving them freedom to do what they have to do to get the project in.

I was discussing success, winning and leadership with a football team; how to make the point? I was standing next to a flipchart, with another chart on the other side of the room. I asked them what they had to do to win at football? They yawned, made rude remarks and laughed. After a few minutes one of them shouted, 'Score more goals than we let in!' – I wrote it down on the flipchart next to me. Another yelled, 'Pass the ball!' – to great laughter from his teammates. I wrote this down as well.

Then, silence.

After a while someone said, with a disparaging voice, 'Speak to each other.' I raced across the room, wrote this down on the other flip chart, and ran back again. I repeated this for the next ten minutes as people started to speak openly. At the end one flip chart had two contributions, (score goals and pass the ball), the other over fifty (belief, communication, attitude, etc.). Jaws on the floor, we started working together.

If you wish to stay on Leadership of Teams, go to **Project Success** 28 (p177)
or
If you wish to change journey, join **Leadership of People**, go to **Inspiration Just Got Real** 36 (p235)

the choice of opposites

You have come from either:

48 – 'Awesome Presentations' (Leadership of Skills)
or
– 'Balance The Sources of Power'
11 (Leadership of Culture)
You are on Leadership of Skills – 6 of 7

Our organisational and personal lives are full of contradictions and opposites. We find them in the words we choose to use, in the way we categorise people and in the cultures of our teams and organisations.

Anthony Robbins writes about the ultimate opposite, in his book *Awaken The Giant Within*, when he writes about pain and pleasure. He believes that all human beings spend all of our lives either moving away from pain or moving towards pleasure. These are the conflicting forces that decide our every thought, decision and action.

Everyone knows the story of whether you see the glass as half full, or half empty, and how this is an indication of whether you are an optimist or a pessimist. This extends into our daily lives with the following opposites. Which ones do you use, pigeon-hole people into, or identify with as being the culture you work in?

1 Which do you say more, 'and' or 'but'?

Sometimes we tend to use 'but' when 'and' is more positive, and powerful. 'But' can be a damaging word.

A friend received a letter from his daughter's next school, which started: 'We hope your daughter is enjoying her final days at her prep school, but is also looking forward to starting with us after the summer.'

So often in our day-to-day lives we can simply replace 'but', with 'and'. It is far more positive, friendly and actually improves how we feel.

2 Do you believe it when you see it, or . . .

See it when you believe it? . . . The first is a well-worn phrase that stops many of us in our tracks, and is the cause of many people giving up, and dreaming a smaller dream. While it may be used as a deliberate put-down, it is more frequently said with no harm intended. The damage may still be done. Over the last few years I have found that unstoppable people say, 'I'll see it when I believe it', each and every day. Massive clue.

3 When talking with your team, do you say 'I', or 'we'?

As a leader, you and your team are in this together, and it is amazing how replacing the simple word 'I' with 'we' shows this. It does not mean you have crossed the barrier from leadership respect to buddy friendship, it does mean you identify with the vision, challenges and thinking of the team. How can you expect others to say 'we' if you do not? Combine this with 'us' instead of 'you', and mean it, and just watch what happens . . .

4 When you want to make change in your life, is it a should, or a must?

There are too many 'shoulds' in our lives – an ineffective word that leads to inaction. The only way real, permanent change takes place is when that 'should' becomes a 'must', an absolute, no alternative, clear, decisive course of action. How many things about your life, in your team, or in your company 'should' change, and how many 'must'?

5 We all work with drains and radiators

And I am not talking about the central heating, or air conditioning, I am talking about people. You know what I mean about a 'drain', I am sure. You spend time with someone, and they are complaining, moaning and generally unhappy. Fair enough, but they never suggest solutions, or positive ways forward, and you suddenly find your strength, your enthusiasm, almost your desire to live, draining out of you.

Of course, it is also draining out of the other person as

well, and both of your combined energies are almost literally disappearing down a drain. What an opposite to radiators – people whose warmth, passion and very presence make us feel warm all over, and fill us with new levels of calm, and personal power. And the irony is, life hits these people just as hard as the drains, but they talk about it in a completely different way. Radiators make the world special just by being in it.

Time for an honesty question: Are you a drain or a radiator?

6 When you listen to your people, team or department, do you hear noise, or music?

One can tell the atmosphere, the environment, of any department, even company, the moment one walks in. It is in the air. So, as a leader, go into the middle of your team, right now, and just experience what is going on around you – is it noise (raised voices, fearful faces, reactive actions) or music (calmness, passion and being proactive)? By the way, you can be calm and still rush around to fix an urgent problem, indeed, it is the most effective state to be in, to achieve the result you wish.

7 Do you ask, 'What's going wrong'? or . . .

What's going well? We automatically move in the direction of our most dominant thoughts. If we choose to look for what is wrong – in a project, in other people, or in ourselves – that is what we will find, and vice versa. Of course that is not to say that we are not aware of events happening that we need to influence or change, but it does put life in perspective. Many projects fail because of this example – they are so busy putting in place risk assessments and contingency plans they have no time, energy or belief in what they were originally setting out to achieve.

Student sitting Oxford University Philosophy exam. The only question: 'Why?'
His only answer: 'Why Not'.
(He scored 100%).

Your story – your choice

One
Once upon a time, there was a large mountainside, where an eagle's nest rested. The eagle's nest contained four large eagle eggs. One day an earthquake rocked the mountain causing one of the eggs to roll down the mountain, to a chicken farm, located in the valley below. The chickens knew that they must protect and care for the eagle's eggs, so an old hen volunteered to nurture and raise the large egg.

One day, the egg hatched and a beautiful eagle was born. Sadly, however, the eagle was raised to be a chicken. Soon, the eagle believed he was nothing more than a chicken. The eagle loved his home and family, but his spirit cried out for more. While playing a game on the farm one day, the eagle looked to the skies above and noticed a group of mighty eagles soaring in the skies. 'Oh,' the eagle cried, 'I wish I could soar like those birds.' The chickens roared with laughter, 'You cannot soar with those birds. You are a chicken and chickens do not soar.'

The eagle continued staring at his real family up above, dreaming that he could be with them. Each time the eagle let his dreams be known, he was told it couldn't be done.

That is what the eagle learned to believe. The eagle, after time, stopped dreaming and continued to live his life like a chicken. Finally, after a long life as a chicken, the eagle closed his eyes and he died.

Two

The great eagle, her huge wings covering the craggy mountain eyrie, was not immediately aware of losing one of her young as she tried to protect them from the fierce storm. The mother hen in the farm below was similarly unaware that something had dropped into the soft hay of her coop.

Reared to behave as a chicken, the young eagle never learned to fly, completely unaware that it was his nature to be a king among birds. A passing hermit noticed him awkwardly holding his great wings while he strutted and pecked with the other chickens.

'Don't you know what you are?' said the hermit, gently taking the eagle in his arms. 'Your nature is to soar the skies. Come stretch forth your wings and fly.'

The hermit's action confused the eagle, however, as he did not know who he was, and he jumped down to rejoin the chickens. For several days the hermit persisted, each time taking the eagle to higher ground, saying, 'Know that, although you may live like a chicken, inside you beats the heart of an eagle, a great eagle; know that you are the king of birds. Go, stretch forth your wings and fly.' But each time, the eagle appeared unaware of his true, unknown self, and awkwardly hopped back to join the chickens who were scratching for corn in the dust. The hermit noticed, though, how the eagle would cast a few glances at the sky, almost as if sensing something stir deep within his heart.

Finally the hermit carried the bird to the top of the

mountain. Reaching a steep crag far above the chicken coop, the hermit held the bird aloft while repeating his words of encouragement. 'Out there, among the heavens is where you belong. Go now! Stretch forth your wings and fly! Become the eagle that you are.'

But still the bird did not accept his true power. Not knowing what to do, the eagle's powerful vision swept back and forth from his coop to the sky. He could see the chickens pecking at their food, and felt that he needed to be back there. Then, as if spying something far in the distance, he began to tremble and slowly stretched out his wings. It seemed to the hermit that the eagle was growing in stature and, just at the moment when he could no longer hold him, the great eagle let out a triumphant cry and soared into the heavens.

Second story from Shooting the Monkey, by Colin Turner.

If you wish to stay on Leadership of Skills, go to **Modelling** 33 (p217)
or
If you wish to change journey, join **Leadership of Team**, go to **Your Personality Becomes Their Personality . . .** 27 (p171)

people mean business
– improve performance
by at least 10%

You have come from either:

37 – 'One Team – One Voice' (Leadership of Teams)
or
– 'Attracting The Headhunters'
38 (Leadership of Career)
You are on Leadership of Teams – 7 of 7

Everyone instinctively knows that igniting the full potential of people is the right thing to do. Following years of money wasting process-driven initiatives, organisations are now waking up to the real crown jewels all around them, their people, and the ideas, innovation and imagination within.

Sadly, so many companies blame their very crown jewels whenever anything goes wrong. If the process doesn't work, someone is to blame. If the organisational structures aren't effective in reality, someone has to pay, and if a project is not delivered, it must be someone's fault. The facts are that structures do not matter, and processes are a convenient excuse.

Many enlightened organisations follow the philosophy that looking after people is all that needs to happen – delighted people = delighted customers. However most companies and leaders need more than this to justify the training, coaching and investments they must make. After all, we know that training is one of the first, and easiest, targets for reduction at budget time.

Management schools throughout the world are giving this issue very serious attention. Indeed, as you read this there will be major theses published, as rival thinkers compete to be the first to be able to stand up and declare – 'We have the formula, and it's ours, and we can license it to you to measure if you are really releasing people's potential.'

In keeping with the Naked Leadership philosophy of cutting through the hype, here are what most of the tomes and analysis will come down to – here are the three ways to know, for certain:

1. **The morale of your team, in a heartbeat;**

2. **The effect on performance and productivity of releasing human potential; and**

3. **The financial and business reasons for which every profit-making organisation exists, and the impact on each by inspired people.**

1 Measuring morale

Never has such a simple process been made so complex. It has become a tree-cutting, paper-driven art form of surveys and analysis. It does not have to be this way:

Like everyone else, your people are driven more by emotion than logic, and yet most organisations run logically driven morale surveys. Morale surveys can be renamed as 'How are you feeling in the moment you are being asked?' (They may feel high because of some non-work related issue, or low because they've just spilled coffee down their clothes.) We need to design a way that takes these into account – and this is exactly how to do it: at a team meeting ask people how they are feeling, right now. Zero means they are very unhappy (suicidal), ten means they feel they can walk on water. Add the total and divide by the number of people present, and presto, you have your finger on the pulse of your team. You decide whether to do the scoring in secret or openly – it depends on the culture. If you do it secretly make sure you say that anyone with a score below two can come and see you at any time.

2 The effect on performance and productivity

People will only ever do anything to the best of their ability for one reason, and one alone, because they want to. (You will be bored with me saying that so often in this book!) There is NO other reason. On average, for every ten people in your organisation there will be three people who will stand by you, no matter what. These people are those whom you can always trust and rely on. At the other end of the spectrum will be two who will always go against you, not publicly, but secretly; these are the negs –

no matter what course of action is suggested, or decisions are made, they will oppose them behind your back, and generally make your life a nightmare. (You will have dealt with the negs on your journey, or they are waiting for you to arrive . . .) In the middle you will have the largest number, five, who will come with you on some things, and not others. These are the people who will determine whether any and all change initiatives work, or fail.

Let's call these three groups, starting with the disenchanted, the negs, the norms and the nice. Now we put a figure on their 'performance' levels, i.e. how much effort, energy and commitment they put into their work, each and every day – remember, this will be entirely governed by them (how much they want to).

Let's say negs perform 25% of their capacity, norms 50% and nice 90%. Your goal is to move as many as you can from negs to norms (say one of two), and from norms to nice (say three of five). Here is the effect of moving these people on your overall performance ratio:

BEFORE	Negs	Norms	Nice	Total
Number	2	5	3	10
Average performance % each	25	50	90	n/a
Total performance (no. × %)	50	250	270	570
Average performance total (570/10)				57%

AFTER	Negs	Norms	Nice	Total
Number	1	3	6	10
Average performance % each	25	50	90	n/a
Total performance (no. × %)	25	150	540	715
Average performance total (715/10)				71.5%

This provides a significant performance improvement of 14.5%! – (71.5 minus 57). So, you can safely say that releasing human potential will improve performance, productivity and results by at least 10%.

3 The financial and business reasons
Every company has specific, bottomline goals, and reasons why they do anything. These can be split between customers and financial.

- **Higher income;**
- **Lower costs;**
- **A balance between the two that provides greater profits;**
- **Higher share-holder value;**
- **More business from existing customers (true measurement of loyalty);**
- **More new customers;**
- **Improved profile and reputation, such as market leader, etc.; and**
- **Helping the wider community.**

As for releasing the potential of your people, should it be on this list? Absolutely, it is at the heart of every single one.

When organisations downsize (reduce their staff numbers) the 'value' of that company increases. For public companies this is reflected in a stock market rise in value, as faceless 'analysts' interpret the loss of people's jobs as good news. This is an absolute nonsense, because whenever a company loses people, which is usually through voluntary redundancy, the first to go are always those they most need to keep.

The first people to volunteer to leave an organisation are always those that are most able to walk into another job, i.e. those with the most skills, confidence and talent. And so the value of these organisations is actually reduced, as they will never be able to shrink to greatness. Add to this the morale of those remaining (rock bottom) and we see why the morale of our people becomes a top priority, every moment of every day.

So next time a company you are investing in reduces its numbers 'on a voluntary basis' be worried about your investment, be very worried indeed.

You have now completed Leadership of Teams, go to **Enlightened Leadership** 42 (p263)
or
If you wish to change journey, join **Leadership of Self**, go to **Ownership – Who's in Charge of You?** 16 (p109)

THE NAKED LEADER

the five pitfalls of leadership

You have come from either:

26 – 'Succession Planning' (Leadership of Career)
or
– 'Leaders Are Born and Not Made!'
10 (Leadership of People)
You are on Leadership of Career – 7 of 7

What are the biggest obstacles to becoming a Naked Leader? The greatest dangers of derailing those who make it? The highest challenges we must rise to, if we are to move beyond what we do, and arrive at what we are?

Mistaking position for Power: Respect has to be earned,

loyalty built. Leaders accept that they work for their people, focusing not on their own achievement, but on the success of others. A leader knows that people working in the front line – on the help desk, for example – make the best day-to-day decisions, and must be empowered to do so. Leaders will never lean on their job title, size of office or position in a hierarchy for authority, or pretend they have access to some greater wisdom not available to others.

Practising communication and not openness: A mistake I have made many times. In their rush to involve others, and become a more communicating department, managers will issue briefings, release documents and shower their teams with e-mails. All in the best possible cause; but in reality, overkill. Different people need different information. Leaders will practise a policy of openness – anyone in their department has a right to ask for any information they wish, and, unless it is company confidential (in which case they will be told why), it will be shared. Also, true openness happens when everyone in an organisation knows exactly where to go to find something out, and they feel they can do this without fear.

If you ask any and every person, team and organisation the one thing that needs to be improved, the word 'communication' will be very high on the list, most often number one. Leaders everywhere must be clear what is meant when people say this – and because communication is itself an ambiguous word (what a paradox!) there is only one sure way to find out what people mean when they ask for more of it – ask them!

Providing answers instead of guidance: They love to show they know the solutions, or the best way to do something. As a result, they jump into someone else's problem with a size ten answer. At best, it will work, and next time they will be asked to help again, and again... Leaders take time to understand the issue, then ask questions to draw out the best way forward. They also follow up to enquire if it was successful and, if it was, they praise – openly.

Putting popularity before respect: We all like to be liked. With your team, however, it can cause major problems. When you become friends with the team that you lead, you cross over the barrier of professional objectivity. Leaders earn respect, and do not worry about being liked.

Being visible, but not available: Visibility is key – knowing the names of your staff and making sure that you walk the department every day. That is not enough – people are no longer motivated by your presence alone, you must also be available for them, in their time, and on their terms. Many leaders are now ensuring personal accessibility to all, at set times, in specific ways. Most people will never take you up on the offer, but they will admire, applaud and respect your actions.

The path of Naked Leadership is never easy, but the rewards are amazing.

One of the mistakes I made in my determination to be 'open' was to copy almost everyone (in a large department) on almost every e-mail I received – big mistake, they wanted to go back to being treated like mushrooms!

Some other classic examples of 'openness', however, may have gone a step too far . . .

'I am sorry for the delays in leaving Woking this morning, the driver has never done this route before and he needs to check which way he is going.' (South West Trains!)

'While you are waiting for your delayed train on the Bakerloo Line, could I just take this opportunity to let you know that during major engineering works the Bakerloo Line will be closed for... 18 months, would you believe. I mean, what are you supposed to do? You could try the Northern Line, but those trains are always ten minutes behind time. You could try the extra buses, but who knows when they will turn up, or where they will go? So, I'm afraid you're rather stuck. Still, if you think you're hard done by, think of me, I have to come in from Slough every day, and that is a nightmare, I can tell you, so good luck to you all, and your delayed train will be here any minute now.' (London Underground Waterloo Station announcement – verbatim – and it got a round of applause from everyone on the platform!)

And on communication generally, we need to be clear exactly what we mean . . .

'I didn't say she stole the money' has six different meanings depending on emphasis placed . . . and . . . When Joe Royle took over as manager of Manchester City, in 1998, they were in the first division. He set his team a clear, unambiguous, very public goal. He said: 'My first priority is to get this team out of this division.' And they achieved that very goal, being relegated to the second . . . and on the London Underground, 'Dogs must be carried.' (No dog, no travel!) . . . and my all-time, personal favourite:

Starbucks Coffee Company – 'If you don't like the way we've made your drink for you, we'll do it again.' (No thanks, can I have one made properly this time!)

You have now completed Leadership of Career, go to **Enlightened Leadership** 42 (p263)
or
If you wish to change journey, join **Leadership of Company**, go to **Job Evaluation in the Bin** 6 (p61)

the most powerful questions on earth
. . . plus . . .

You have come from either:

30 – 'The Fastest Way to Make Any Change in Your Life' (Leadership of Self)
or
50 – 'The 7 Greatest Conspiracies of Success' (Leadership of Career)
You are on Leadership of Self – 5 of 7

Questions

① **If you could do anything in your life, and know that you could not fail, what would you do? Who would you be?** A question inspired in me by Jack Canfield's life-changing book, *Chicken Soup For The Soul*. It made me think, it led me to redefine failure as giving up. Since then I have never given up on the important 'musts' in my life, and so I have never failed. You can do exactly the same, and it is far more than just redefining a word, it is redefining what it means to fail. How can we fear something that can never happen?

Thank you Jack, on behalf of everyone who has taken this on board.

2. **How would you see that if you were the other person?** This is a relationship, reality and rapport question, all in one. It helps us understand each other, it makes us realise there are more realities than just our own, and it helps people become closer. A good supplementary question is, 'Are this person's motives good, or bad?'

This works so powerfully in our personal relationships. Often, after years of being together, the spark can dampen, if not disappear. By taking an interest, a genuine interest, in each other's view of life, magic happens . . .

3. **What are you personally going to do about it?** A stand-up-and-be-counted question. So often we blame 'them', or we say we feel strongly about something but do nothing about it. This was a question that hit me first when I was seventeen. Patrick Meehan had been imprisoned for a crime committed in my hometown of Ayr, and I was convinced by many people he was innocent. I was telling a friend how I felt about it, and he asked me that question. It made me stand up and act . . .

4. **What do you think about . . . (add an issue, an event or a subject)?** A wonderful question for negs at work. Think about it – everyone has an opinion, so it is a question that

is impossible to avoid. And if they try to by saying, 'I don't know', or similar, simply say, 'OK, please think about it for 24 hours and then we can have another chat about it.'

Simply brilliant question! (Make sure you go back though!!)

5 **What exactly has to happen to ensure we achieve this result?** WOW – You want to be a hero in any meeting, in any conversation with your boss, or project. I was once in a difficult project review – over 20 people arguing and desperately competing to gain the attention of our chief executive (and this meeting was in German!) The only eleven words I used in the entire meeting were: *'Was muss passieren dass wir dieses Ergebnis erzielen?'* (What must happen to ensure we achieve the result?)

Even now, two years later, people still comment on my contribution to that project!

6 **What is the specific outcome we are looking to achieve?** When we talk about outcomes, people think 'tangible deliverables', as opposed to all of the intangibles that so many projects have been hiding behind for too many years. This question also makes us look at what we want to achieve, not what we have to avoid.

I was in a meeting, discussing a public sector project that was in trouble, and edging towards disaster. The room was full of people allocating blame like some grossly negative poisonous pie chart, and the facilitator called a break for coffee (to drink, although some people wanted to throw it around). There was a moment's silence (calling for a break is a brilliant way of changing the 'state' of an argument) and the facilitator made this statement: 'It might be useful for us all to think about the specific outcome we are looking to achieve.' It was the turning point for the project.

(7) **And by far the most powerful, to change our lives . . . for anything and everything (ask it anytime, every day, and watch your life change): How does this event help me/us to achieve . . .?** What we think about, we are, what we focus on, we will become. No event has any meaning other than the meaning we choose to give it. Combine all three and you have this amazing question . . .

Hugh Macken is one of the best project managers I have ever met. One of his favourite questions in project turnarounds, is this very question. I have seen amazing reactions – he has stood in front of project teams for the first time, apparently facing a project showstopper, and with project managers who have given up.

Words

There are three words that are so powerful, their impact is awesome. In order:

(1) **A person's name**: Dale Carnegie told us this years ago in his definitive work, *How to Win Friends and Influence People*. The single sweetest word, or sound, in the whole of this world, is that of our own name. So, use people's names, and see the difference. Also, avoid the much-used 'there' as a name-substitute. Thus we will no longer have to endure: 'Hello there, how are you?' . . . ugh!

(2) **'Would'. (With thanks to John Gray, *Men are from Mars, Women are from Venus, Children Are from Heaven*)**: Picture the scene. It's bedtime for your son or daughter. You say 'It's bedtime now, Michael, can you go to bed please?'

Michael's subconscious thinks, 'Can I go to bed, am I physically capable of doing this? Yes, but I am watching TV at
the moment, thank you very much...' or 'Rebecca, will you
tidy your bedroom?' Rebecca thinks, 'Will I, now she is asking me to predict the future, which I am unable to do...' or
'Claire, could you pick up that ice cream wrapper please?'
Claire ponders, 'Could I, now he doubts my ability to...'
etc. etc.

The word 'would' – to adults as well as children, is
powerful because it gives over command of the position,
ownership of the request, to the other person, in a way that
does not in any way doubt their abilities. By the way, this
is not political correctness gone mad, it is the way that we
think as human beings . . .

3 **'Because . . .'**: An amazing word, provided a reason
follows. When we are asked to justify anything, as leaders,
people most often want to know *why* we are asking them
to do something. Providing this ensures people are with us,
it wins over doubters and takes us all forward. People will
only ever do something to the best of their abilities for one
reason, and one alone, *because* they want to.

Phrases

1 **To destroy a blame culture, forever . . .**: 'It's my fault.'
Awesome! I used this in a team once, saying that if anything went 'wrong' it was my fault as leader (and they were
to say this as often as they wished, to whoever they chose)
and if things went well, praise was always to be allocated
to someone else. This will not only eliminate a blame
culture, it will earn you a respect with your people that is
beyond description.

The most moving moment of my working life was when a team of over forty people encircled me in a pub, to celebrate one of their many successes. All they did was shout, 'Leader, leader'. If any of you are reading this, thank you, you did it yourselves.

A word of caution on this. I don't know what the dress code is in your place of work, but for the first week that you do this, wear one of those American Football outfits, with helmet. You'll need it. After a week, you can go naked . . .

2 **To instantly get another person to see your side of any argument**: When we are trying to persuade someone else of our opinion, this is what we normally do . . .

We make our point.
They make their point.
We disagree with their point, and make ours again.
They disagree with ours, and make theirs again.

This would be all exceedingly boring if the points were not being made with passion, so fortunately the conversation is far from boring, unfortunately though, it is proving very, very draining for both of us. And we carry on doing this, the things we have always been doing, always expecting a different result.

If this has ever happened to you, and you decide to break out of this vicious cycle, and into a victorious one, there is a phrase that will ensure they see your point of view, and it is... 'I'm sorry (name), you're completely right.' The first thing the other person will say (after a pause, and providing you have said this with genuine feeling) will be something like: 'No no, I can see your point as well.' Something you have been trying to persuade them of; all along . . .

A close professional friend of mine, James, phoned me and said that he had been in dispute with one of his peers, Tim, about the next action to take on a project. He thought one approach was right, his colleague thought a different route was right. It had been going on for several weeks with no progress towards resolution. I suggested he use the phrase. He objected, loudly, pointing out that this other person was not right, far from it. I suggested again that, if he truly wanted to resolve this and move forward, he should use the phrase.

Two hours later he phoned again, to report the amazing result, they had reached agreement. Why does this work? This is probably what happened between James and Tim: 'James: 'I think we should bring in more business expertise.' Tim: 'It's not more business expertise we need, it's more technical knowledge.' (Pause) James: (probably after a deep breath) 'I'm sorry, Tim, you're completely right.' (Long Pause) Tim: 'No, no James, I can see your point as well.'

If you wish to stay on Leadership of Self, go to **Living as a Leader** 2 (p39)
or
If you wish to change journey, join **Leadership of People**, go to **Leadership in Times of War** . . . 49 (p313)

awesome presentations

You have come from either:

14 – 'Influence in Company Meetings'
(Leadership of Skills)
or
34 – 'Hidden Account Management'
(Leadership of Company)
You are on Leadership of Skills – 5 of 7

There are so many beliefs about presentations:

- **People would rather die than give a presentation (really?):**
- **If you are not feeling sick with worry before a presentation, you are not properly prepared (I beg your**

pardon?); and, my personal favourite
Presenters are born, and not made (people are born, not made).

One of the reasons that such 'truths' fester is because there has been so much written about the mechanical side of giving a presentation and the process of preparation, whereas, important though they are, they will not help you be the hero that you can be. And it is hero status you must seek if you are to make a huge impact, and influence your audience.

The way to achieve this is in four steps:

Step 1 Understand that presentations are an emotional experience

From the moment you are asked to deliver one, to several months and years afterwards (perhaps all of your life). That's step one done then. Not convinced?

OK – let's say you are asked to give a presentation to your Board of Directors. It is a very, very important presentation. You are asked on 4th February if you can give the presentation to the May Board meeting, three months later. What happens next?

A You acknowledge the opportunity, and plan your timings. You will do the research during February, prepare the presentation in March, and make any last minute changes, as well as rehearsing, in April. That way you do not have to even think about the presentation until the day it is being delivered, which you do, and then you forget about it, other than the specific actions that have been agreed as a result of your talk. Or . . .

B You acknowledge the opportunity, and your feelings take over. You wonder what will happen if you make a mistake, screw up or if the day is a disaster. Yes, you still do your research, by day, but by night you lie awake going through the talk over and over and over and over and over again. And when you do drift into sleep, the nightmares start . . . Oh no, it's March. Yes, you prepare your overheads, but still, each and every moment, you worry, as every second brings the moment closer. Then it's April. You start rehearsing it in your mind, and that doesn't help because you can't prepare for everything, for all those questions... come the day, you are already on the tablets to pep you up and seal you up! You give the talk, then you ask yourself the one question that everyone asks, 'What was I like?' (By the way, if anyone ever asks you this question about themselves, straight after a talk, the correct answer is, 'You were great, well done.') . . . And then the emotion and nightmares continue for several months. Indeed, although most people praised you, they were only saying these things to be nice, you are much more interested in those one or two things that went wrong . . .

Now, as I say many times in this book, there is no right or wrong, there is only what serves you, and what does not. So, it's your choice, which serves you, A, or B?

Step 2 Take control of your state

Think about all of the amazing presentations you have given, or, better still, imagine giving a fantastic presentation. Remember, our minds cannot tell the difference between something that happens in 'reality' and something we imagine with emotional intensity, so visualize how brilliant you will be, be there, in the event, at its centre. Feel the energy. (By the way, if you've met Your Centre on your journey, put yourself in the optimum state. If not, Your Centre awaits you with huge warmth, friendship and good feeling, somewhere on your path ahead . . .)

Step 3 Focus on only one type of content – what's in it for your audience?

That is all they will care about – what's in it for them? So know your Board well, research where the company is going and speak with a few of them beforehand to 'ask their advice on this subject' (they will be chuffed). I am not saying you simply tell them what they want to hear, I am saying you share with them how what you are proposing will achieve their outcome. It's just like any sales situation – people hate to be sold to, but we love to buy.

Step 4 Speak with passion

The critical question any audience, from one to one hundred thousand, will ask themselves, about you, is this – does this person believe what they are saying? If you do not, do not say it. If you do, say it like you do. When you do this, eye contact becomes automatic, passion kicks in, and charisma takes over.

And that's it – yes, give it a structure, yes, make the content sizzle, but most importantly be you, believe in what you say and say it so that your audience can see the real benefits for them.

Outstanding presenters I know do not present, they give a dramatic performance. And I am not just referring to the big event, when presenting to just a few people, the more you give of yourself, the more effective the message. However, that is not all. When we communicate we have our appearance, voice and content. What is the relative impact of each?

- *appearance – 57%*
- *voice – 36%*
- *content – 7%*

(By the way, these figures apply to every communication we make – we can substitute 'words' for 'content'.)

* * *

I believe that Nigel Risner is the best speaker in the world. He excites, he challenges, and he ensures people take action. He knows that action is everything, and it is. I asked Nigel to share one single message that makes the difference between an average presenter, and an awesome one:

'In order for your message to INSPIRE INTO ACTION, it needs to be done in a manner in which your audience, however big or small, feel that it was delivered personally to them, each one of them. Many times when I have spoken, someone will come up to me and say, "that was so spot on, how did you know that about me?" Then I know I have delivered, and you can too . . .'

If you wish to stay on Leadership of Skills, go to **The Choice of Opposites** 44 (p279)
or
If you wish to change journey, join **Leadership of Career**, go to **The 7 Greatest Conspiracies of Success** 50 (p319)

THE NAKED LEADER

leadership in times of war . . .

You have come from either:

3 – 'Our Secret Driving Forces' (Leadership of People)
or
– 'The Most Powerful Questions on Earth . . .
47 Plus . . .' (Leadership of Self)
You are on Leadership of People – 2 of 7

When we are asked to name great leaders, we are likely to have wartime examples in our list, which might include Churchill, Napoleon and Rommel. In the past business people have said there is little crossover between the world of work, and the world of war . . . until now.

The characteristics of great military leaders include the

ability to think and act quickly in very fast-changing environments, to focus on survival at all times and, of course, the ability to motivate people in high pressure and stressful times. Not unlike the situation that faces leaders today. In the business world, our experience does not extend to life or death, but increasingly, the similarity of skills, strategies and action needed in war are being identified as those required in today's fast moving, turbulent, uncertain times.

With this in mind, I went back in history to a particular conflict, much researched and talked about for the skills of its leaders, namely the US Civil War, and in particular the Southern Generals. Historians are united on one conclusion, the South, vastly outnumbered, with inferior firearms and no clear long-term goal, only lasted as long as they did as a fighting force because of the thinking, actions and inspiration of their leaders. What lessons can leaders and teams learn from looking at three Southern Generals, namely Lee, Longstreet and Stewart?

General Lee

General Lee was an officer in the US Army, and he was actually offered field command of the US Army by President Lincoln. In 1861, when war threatened, he turned it down in favour of commanding his beloved South. He commanded the Southern armies throughout the war, and allegedly knew the name of every officer under his command (over 400). Lee is now regarded as the most beloved war leader in American history, despite the fact that he dedicated his military life to the secession.

General Lee taught us some valuable lessons on who we are, and who we can be:

- People will believe in you as a leader if they believe your heart is in what you are doing – if you do not enjoy what you are doing, you will be found out.
- Belief – Lee instilled a deep and passionate belief in his people, at every level, from politician to infantryman.
- Charisma – Lee had total charisma – character, personality and presence. Don't let anyone tell you these things don't matter, they do, in spades.

General Longstreet

Longstreet was Lee's most trusted soldier, his right arm. His defensive theories were years ahead of their time. He believed in focusing on the mission, and only on the mission. If fighting could be avoided, all the better. If Longstreet had been listened to at the decisive Battle of Gettysburg, America would now be two countries.

We can learn a great deal about crisis management from General Longstreet.

- Focus on the outcome, on what you want to achieve – not on what you don't want to achieve. Be absolutely clear on this.
- Within that, focus on the important issues, those that take you closer to your desired end-game, put aside the trivial, ignore the unimportant.
- Deploy people according to their strengths – be aware of your team's natural talents, and use these to the maximum if things go wrong.

General Stewart

Jeb Stewart was the eyes and ears of the Southern army.

His cavalry would ride for weeks on dangerous missions into enemy territory, and his men would often infiltrate Union bars and camps to gain vital information on specific subjects, seeking the key information his generals needed to know, when they needed to know it. Many of the early Southern victories would have been lost without the inside knowledge of Stewart.

Stewart was an early advocate of knowledge management, (that's real management of knowledge, not the hype that so many consultants hide behind today), and competitor analysis.

- **Knowledge management is useless without a definition of what information we need, and it must relate to your vision, aims and agenda.**
- **Proactive teams must anticipate information that is required, and provide it ahead of it being requested.**
- **To truly understand our competitors, we must put ourselves in their shoes, and see the business world as they see it. How often do you do this?**

Leaders face many challenges, and so much change, in scale, scope and speed. We have to think and act fast, and such ongoing 'crisis' management calls for leadership skills that can often be learned from military history.

At leadership seminars I always ask for the names of 'great' leaders. (I always say 'great' and never define it.) In the United Kingdom . . .

- *One name always comes up, every time.*
- *One name always causes a storm of disagreement, when it is offered.*

- *One name never came up at all before 2001, and is now mentioned every time.*

Stop reading and write down your list of 'great' leaders.

'Great' Leaders

....
....
....
....
....
....

Ok, here are those names:

- *Always comes up, every time – Adolf Hitler.*
- *Causes a storm of disagreement, when it is offered – Margaret Thatcher. (Much more than Hitler!)*
- *One name never came up at all before 2001, and is now mentioned every time (Jesus Christ) – another indication of the enlightenment, spiritual revolution that is starting to happen.*

If you wish to stay on Leadership of People, go to
Inspiration Just Got Real 36 (p235)
or
If you wish to change journey, join **Leadership of Teams**,
go to **Your Team – From Good to Unstoppable** 15 (p103)

the 7 greatest conspiracies of success

You have come from either:

1
    – 'The Structure of Guaranteed Success'
    or
    – 'Awesome Presentations' (Leadership of Skills)

48
    You are on Leadership of Career – 1 of 7
    (Leadership of Career)

The formula for success is simple, clear and guaranteed. So why do so many people not achieve the 'success' they desire and deserve? One reason is the conspiracies – the lies of success which prevent us being all that we can be.

These are the seven most influential conspiracies, in

reverse order of destructiveness, and exactly what to do about each:

7 We need permission to be successful

Often stemming from childhood, we crave approval for what we do. When we finish a presentation, there is only one question on our minds, 'What was I like?' Many people spend their lives in a sort of abeyance, waiting for someone to set them free.

You do not need permission to be successful, and if you do, photocopy this page and carry this 'success ticket' with you wherever you go:

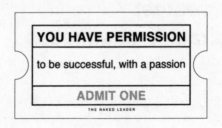

YOU HAVE PERMISSION

to be successful, with a passion

ADMIT ONE

THE NAKED LEADER

6 'Make me a woman'

Whenever anybody suggests that we can be anything we want to be, those people who do not believe this, immediately go off the Richter scale. They start to ask for things that they consider to be impossible to happen. They do this, not because they actually want to achieve these ambitions, but rather to win an argument that we cannot be anything that we want to be, after all.

The great sadness is they are actually convincing themselves, against themselves, i.e. running down their own strengths, ability and potential. The great irony of this is that, more often than not, they will suggest things that actually are possible. Some real-life examples:

- 'I want to be one of the first members of the public to go up in a space shuttle.'
- 'I want to have the best memory in the world.'
- 'I want to be taller.'
- 'Make me a woman.' (It was a man requesting this, by the way!)

And I can list scores more.

Whenever I meet these suggestions, first of all I establish whether this is what the person really, really wants. When they think about these dreams, does their heart soar? More often than not, the answer is sadly no. I say 'sadly' because I would love to help people achieve what they consider to be impossible. Because, in fact, all of the four listed outcomes are possible.

And when I suggest this, the other person will often accuse me of avoiding their point, which is not, 'Can you help me achieve my dreams?', but is, 'You can't help me be anything I want to be, because that is impossible.'

Now this is deep stuff, but it is right at the heart of human ambition, and one of the main reasons that people do not strive higher. Because when we are convinced that we cannot be anything we want to be, we decide not to be much more than we already are.

The scales of achievement are firmly tipped towards fear of failure, conformity and lack of inner belief. By suggesting you can be anything you want to be, I am rebalancing your scales of possibility, and inviting you to move away from words such as 'achievable', and 'realistic'.

And here is another key point, namely, 'fear of success'.

Many people will challenge this because of fear of failure, and others will do so because of fear of success. For to succeed may mean change (and we are all very uncomfortable with change), it may mean action, or leaving something behind.

Other times, people will genuinely suggest things that cannot be achieved:

- 'I want to play football for England in the next World Cup.' (This is a 56-year-old lady speaking.)
- 'To fly across Britain, unaided by artificial supports such as wings or in a plane.'
- 'To live forever.'

And so the list goes on.

Clearly there are some results that are impossible to achieve. And so, once again, when people name these, I ask them if that is what they really, really want. And once again, most people say no, that they are simply proving a point.

And, get this. In all my experience of working with leaders, with teams and with organisations, I have **never**, that's **never** met anyone who **REALLY WANTED** to achieve anything that was impossible.

Because, when our minds start to open up to the possibility that we really can make our wildest dreams come true, when we think just for a moment about the awesome possibilities that we can achieve in our lives, when our hearts open up to the life we would love to live, our automatic defence mechanism kicks in.

It tells us we cannot achieve any of these things, and to 'prove' it, tells us there are many things in life we cannot achieve, and that the one that we really, really want must be on that list.

In fact, life is full of people who take the opposite view completely. When any part of themselves, or anyone else, says, 'You can't,' or, 'You won't,' they simply say, 'I don't believe you, I won't believe you, I cannot be true to myself if I believe you.'

And guess what happens?

You don't need to ask.

And so, I invite you, next time anyone says to you that you could be anything you want to be, instead of focusing on the *anything*, focus on the *want* as well.

5 If I am to be successful, someone else has to fail – there is not enough success to go around

As Homer Simpson would say, 'Doh!' – because this is the 'I must beat myself up because I'm doing well' approach.

In fact, this is one of the most dangerous, damaging and destructive beliefs we can ever have. This one stems from how we measure whether we are being successful, in the first place. The question to ask yourself is, how do you measure success, or judge whether you are being successful? Now, I used to think that people did this not by looking at how much 'happiness' or 'money' or 'whatever' they had, personally, but by comparing their amount of 'success' with other people. This is very damaging in itself, and it gets worse. I am now convinced that this is wrong, we do not judge our success by how successful other people are, but by how successful *we think* they are. Critical difference.

Think of someone you have labeled as 'happy', has a wonderful life or who enjoys each and every day. How do you know? The answer is we do not. I personally know many leaders who have achieved amazing success, *by my standards*, and yet when I get to know them better, I dis-cover they are actually very unhappy.

The only sane, measurable and calming way to decide if you are being successful is to ask yourself whether you are moving closer to your dream, or aim, or purpose, whatever you choose to call it, or whether you are moving further away. And, by the way, when people comment on your success or progress or life, they are only doing this from their own perspective (they can do it from no other).

Your success, no one else's.

Because only some people achieve what they deem to be success, we assume that success is in short supply, a scarce commodity. Indeed, it is, but not for the reason you might think. Because success is personal to us as human beings, definitions of success will be totally different for each of us. So there is indeed a shortage of success for us as individual human beings, a shortage that is one – ours! However, as we only need one success (at a time) one is also a plentiful number.

And there is everything wonderful in expressing your own personal success, as you wish. So, before you caution yourself not to be special, not to be different, not to achieve amazing things, ask yourself, would Tina Turner have had such a big hit with *Simply The Average?* Or, just imagine the Olympic TV programme – *Going for Bronze*. And think about that lesser known hit by Queen – *We are The Runners-Up*.

By the way, there is plenty of success to choose from; the volume of success is positively overwhelming. Go into any large bookshop and you will find hundreds of books, we can buy them at railway stations, motorway service stations, on tape, on CD ROM . . .

Our biggest challenge is actually reducing the success

guidance to achieve our own definition of success (this book is designed to help you do just that).

4 Cultures

We are all brought up in different ways, but our cultural upbringing has an enormous impact on whether we achieve what we want in life, or not. I am not talking about whether we are born into money or wealth, or a certain class, I am talking about the key cultural messages we received when we were younger. When you were young, and you announced you wanted to be an 'inventor' or a 'train driver' or 'famous', or whatever, did your parents manage your expectations? Did they say, 'You won't be able to do that, because…'? Please be clear, they did it out of love for you, because they did not want you to reach too high, fall over and be hurt.

It is very different these days; when children say they want to work in a shop, be an actor or actress, or anything, most parents encourage them by saying how great they will be at whatever they have 'chosen'.

And of course, the difference between these two approaches is that one will have few choices open to them when they come to decide what to do, while the other will have an unlimited choice.

By the way, when children say they are going to be something, when they grow older, they usually change their minds within a few hours, so we may as well encourage them! Children and adults alike have to negotiate this culture of conformity. This is a rule that surrounds us every day, and pulls us, like a magnet, towards the majority of people around us. Because it feels safe, because we like to be liked, because we can all be the same.

Breaking free of cultural differences is not easy, but it is, once again, your choice. It simply does not serve those around you to think small, to hold your head low, to not reach for more. I was working in a hospice and speaking with a lady who had only a few days to live. Quite apart from the fact that everyone saw her as 'dying' whereas to me she was very much 'living', it was her openness about life that struck me. One afternoon she said to me, 'Do you know, David, I believe a person's biggest regret, when it is their time to leave this life, is not the things they did, and did wrong, but those things they wanted to do, and never started.'

The saddest words in existence are, 'If only, it might have been'.

What are you going to do, right now, that culture has stopped you from doing?

- **Tell your partner of many years that you love them, and mean it.**
- **Hold your son or daughter that bit closer, and tell them they can be anything they want to be.**
- **Go to visit your mum or dad and tell them you love them, whether or not they told you when you were younger, because they probably did.**

In the United Kingdom we also face cultural issues in business. If organisations are very successful and make a profit this can be frowned upon, and the people who made it happen, called 'fat cats'. When this happens the papers quote the Bible, saying that money is 'the root of all evil', which is an incorrect quote, the Bible actually says (1 Timothy 6:10) '. . . the love of money is a root of all kinds of evil'.

However, if companies lose money and have to make job losses that is also unacceptable.

Finally, if people fail in business and go bankrupt that is seen as the ultimate failure.

And so anyone embarking on being all they can be, in business terms, needs thick skin, colossal humility and to learn the following phrases:

- **When things are going well – 'I'm so lucky'.**
- **When things are not going so well – 'I must be mad'.**

3 Focusing on what we do not want

These are the four most destructive words in our language – please, please, never say these words to any other human being, or think them about yourself.

'You have something missing.'

Why so damaging? Quick course in human psychology: as human beings we do not think in negatives, we cannot. When we think about a negative, we always focus on the positive.

Right now, wherever you are, do not think of a blue banana – you had to think about the blue banana, before telling yourself not to think about it.

There are hundreds of similar examples:

- **Handing a hot plate to a child and saying, 'Don't touch the plate, it's hot.'**

- **Alton Towers Oblivion, vertical drop rollercoaster – as you hang, suspended in your car just before plummeting underground, what do they say? 'Don't look down' . . . and what does everyone do?**

- I overheard a mother giving a crystal clear instruction to her son in the park: 'Don't you dare not do what I told you to.'

- I was on a train sitting next to a chap who took a mobile call from what was obviously his wife/partner. It was a crowded train, we were squashed up close, and I could hear both sides of the conversation:

    Woman (in alarm) – 'Darling, the mortgage forms haven't arrived yet, what are we going to do?' (Note – she was upset, and she was asking what they should do, not what they should not do – an excellent start to a useful conversation.)

    Man – 'Don't panic.' (Telling her what not to do.)

    Woman (now in great alarm, and shouting) – 'I'm not panicking, don't you tell me not to panic.' (A request not to repeat what her partner has said previously, as it may not assist a positive exchange between them.)

    Man – 'I said, don't panic.' (Hint – she knows what you said, she even asked you not to say it again. She did not ask you to repeat what you said).

    Woman (now hysterical) – 'I'm not listening to you telling me not to panic . . .'

    And the rest of the conversation featured some choice words which I will not repeat here.

These everyday examples are full of 'don'ts' always leading to the exact opposite. So, if we are to achieve what we want in life, we must focus on what we want. It is no good saying you don't want a blame culture in your organisation, or you don't want so many reports or you don't want… ask yourself, what do you want? And when you've done that, perhaps this weekend, go off and look for some-

THE NAKED LEADER

thing missing – you will have a field day looking around for something that is not there. Enjoy!

One final point on negatives – if they are emphasised too much, because our minds do not think in negatives, they can become a huge, driving instruction to do the opposite.

- **You may identify with being told you would 'never' achieve something, over and over, and it drove you to ensure you went out and did achieve it.**

- **Telling our children over and over, not to do something (in particular if we add, because it is 'bad', or add a similar label that they can interpret as 'exciting').**

- **Pointing out that a work document that we have brought home must not be touched because it is 'very, very important and private'. (Cue to children to show massive interest in something they would have otherwise ignored.)**

A classic example of the second point, was a friend of mine, aged 12 watching TV with his mum and dad – it was Morecambe and Wise. A stripper appeared, and his mum rushed up to turn off the television. She turned round and said, 'You must never, ever, ever, show any interest in seeing women take off their clothes, it is very, very wrong.'

I think he is cured now, but last time I saw him, when he was at university in Edinburgh, he spent every moment of his spare time . . . I think you get the picture.

2 You have to believe it, for it to work
The biggest con of the global training industry – the king's

new clothes of conspiracies. If I adopted this I would say to you, something like: 'The stuff in this book will only work if you believe it.' You would put one of the ideas into action, and it might not work for you, so you would e-mail me. I would reply: 'It didn't work because you didn't believe it strongly enough. I told you, it only works if you believe it, now go away and do some more believing.'

I know too many people who make a living on this basis, they have surrendered their own accountability, and it is very, very sad. I do not care one whit if you believe what is in this book, or not. I don't care whether you believe in me as an author, or as an idiot, I DO care, WITH PASSION, that you go out and take action. End of story.

Key point: this conspiracy refers to whether you believe what others tell you about leadership and being all that you can be. There is one key test of everything we can read, be told or learn about leadership – does it work for us? This type of belief is different from believing in yourself. Such belief, in your own abilities, strengths and all that you can do are absolutely critical to your success.

And at number one, not a new entry, it's been around a while, and it's the one the negs thrive on, the single most destructive lie . . .

1 Just wait until reality catches up

The winner of all conspiracies, the ultimate lie. It basically says, look, you set out on your fool's journey if you want, but know this, sooner or later reality will bring you tumbling down . . .

One morning, on a phone-in on Radio 5 Live, the presenter said, 'Do you not think Everton are now playing at their own level, that they are back in touch with reality?'

No, Everton are playing at the level that their present team play at, nothing more, nothing less. Put eleven different players on the pitch and you would have a different 'reality'.

Let's say there are a million people reading this book right at this very moment (OK, so I'm an optimist), while you are all reading exactly the same words, you are all, every single one of you, interpreting them differently, you are interpreting them for your own life. We have not one reality, we have one million different realities. Because none of these words I am writing have any meaning whatsoever, other than the meaning you choose to give them. By the way, that is also true of every event in our lives.

So . . . be aware of these different interpretations, these alternative possibilities, these many meanings, and simply choose the reality that serves you best. And when I say 'serves you best', I mean select the reality that takes you closer to achieving your own, personal success.

When people wake up to these conspiracies, and banish them forever, we take a leap that very few make . . .

There is one question in the English language that in the United Kingdom we ask each other each and every day, but we do not actually want an answer. That question is: 'How are you?' Most of us reply, 'Not too bad' (see 3 above!), and others say something like, 'Fine' or, 'Bit of a headache', etc. and then we move on, and so does life. The person asking is only being polite, of course, and so are we in our reply. Seldom do more meaningless discussions take place.

Now, if you want to break this mould of conformity and thinking in the negative, all in one, answer like this (with vast enthusiasm, energy and while making direct eye contact); 'I'm REALLY glad you asked me that. Things are going AMAZINGLY well for me, thank you very much. My job is FANTASTIC, my partner and I are SO IN LOVE, my children are models of what every child should be, and if I was any happier, I'D BE TWINS.'

I am of course emphasising for effect – you might want to find a half-way approach to this. After all, the person you first speak with in this way may well never speak with you again!

If you wish to stay on Leadership of Career, go to **The Power of Mentoring** 5 (p53)
or
If you wish to change journey, join **Leadership of Self**, go to **The Most Powerful Questions on Earth . . . Plus . . .** 47 (p299)

leadership by e-mail

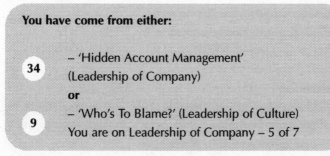

You have come from either:

34
– 'Hidden Account Management'
(Leadership of Company)
or
9
– 'Who's To Blame?' (Leadership of Culture)
You are on Leadership of Company – 5 of 7

How did we ever manage without e-mail? How did people cope without our daily fix of words, communication and information?

Many people argue they have simply replaced the old-fashioned internal memo, the ones that were often colour coded to indicate their importance. Wrong. E-mail has completely revolutionised communication, on the one hand becoming core to doing business, on the other a sort of electronic drug addiction. Our in-trays seem to act like magnets, speeding up the tempo, complexity and reactive pressure of business life.

They also said that e-mail would herald the end of paper, as we move towards the paper-free office. Wrong again, as indicated by the growth in paper as everyone prints them off. For some time to come we will trust a physical piece of paper more than anything 'online'. We can hold a piece of paper, it makes us feel secure, whichever pile it chooses to then hide in.

However, the biggest concern about e-mail is its impact on communications. E-mails feed our reactive, rather than responsive behaviour, often failing to make the points intended, and too often used as an alternative to other means of contact. As one of the most public, powerful and prevalent forms of corporate communication, there is a need for caution, care and clarity.

And so here is a top ten guide for leadership by e-mail. Become a genuine, caring Naked Leader by e-mail.

1. **Be aware of the impact of the written word, always far greater than other forms of communication. It is direct, to the point and often comes across as aggressive. To more than overcome this, make your e-mails friendly (write 'Dear name', and always end on a friendly note, avoiding 'Kind Regards'). Use 'we' rather than 'you' and always put yourself in the place of the recipient – reading through what you have written before you send it.**

2. **Never (that's never) send an e-mail reply when you are angry – it starts a negative spiral that can be difficult to**

break. Write out the mail, by all means, but rather than send it, hold it in abeyance until you are calmer.

3 Avoid copy-copy disease. So, how do you react when you receive:

To: M Burton
cc: The whole board, the entire management team, everyone in the post room
Mike
Your department is useless, and so are you
Best Wishes
Tom

or equivalent?

A friend of mine calls these the 'three hour' e-mails – it takes her three hours to sort! If you are sent one of these, hard as it may be, only reply to the person writing.

4 Be absolutely crystal clear in your e-mail – if personal communications can lead to misunderstanding, that is nothing to the confusion that e-mail can cause. This is a genuine one I received before I opened a conference – from the chief executive of the company.

David
Just to confirm I will be introducing you tomorrow at 9 a.m.
You've got a lot to learn
Ian

I remember reading it through again and again, *You've got a lot to learn* seemed a bit rude, especially as he and I had never even met! I phoned him up to thank him for the note, confirm arrangements, and as casually as I could enquired about the meaning of this sentence, to which he replied: 'Well you have got a lot to learn David, I've seen your script, 12 pages long – I don't know how you do it . . . I'm very impressed.' Aha!!!

5. Never give bad news of any kind by e-mail.

6. Never include information on other companies in e-mails. Such detail can, and has been, used in courts of law. Do not use e-mail to discuss competitors, potential acquisitions or mergers, or to give your opinion about another company. The word 'confidential' simply does not apply to electronic communication; somebody else in your organisation can always access it. (See also 10 below.)

7. Beware with information on individuals. Take great care, even with facts. Also, avoid providing references by e-mail.

8. Personal e-mails. Many companies are concerned about the growing numbers of non-work-related correspondence. Often these will be through in-house bulletin boards. The key words here are guidelines and trust. Put in place a clear policy that gives some freedom, but let people know their boundaries on time and content. There is a difference between such personal e-mails, and personalising business correspondence.

9. It is one thing to misunderstand the sender's intent, quite another to deliberately attack someone by e-mail. Business bullying is now recognised by industrial tribunals as a form of illegal behaviour in itself. Another form of bullying that is on the increase is the chain e-mail. These are at best unpleasant and at worst destructive in terms of

time, volume of traffic and personal well-being.

You know the sort of thing:

'Send this to 10 people within an hour of reading it or you will receive bad luck.'

Simple solution, if you are worried about these, send them to david@nakedleader.com and I'll take the risks.

10 **Electronic communications are no different from every other form, and there should be no need for complex guidelines, rules and restrictions. As long as everyone is clear on your company's policy, none of these potential dangers will grow out of hand. People must take personal ownership of their e-mails, even after pressing Send.**

E-mail needs a balance between leadership and corporate control. Many organisations do not realise that, whilst their people use the corporate e-mail system for both personal and business correspondence, the content in these e-mails can render both the company and the person sending the e-mail liable to litigation. Added to this issue is the legal framework that could have a board member attending a court of law in defence of an e-mail abuse activity within his or her company.

The answer to minimising the risk of legal exposure to today's corporate board member is threefold – individual responsibility, clear policy and external auditing. Your responsibility as an individual is clear in some areas – you know the difference between right and wrong. However there are huge holes here, ones that can only be filled by a clear, concise and compelling policy.

To have an effective corporate policy means establishing a policy group which would consist of the HR director to cover all legal issues (such as informing staff of the policy), the security director (addressing the issue of e-mail archiving and lockdown), the technical consultant for implementation of the policy and, of course, it should be chaired by the IT director.

First step – put a policy in place (invite people to contribute and be involved in its content).

Second step – ensure it is understood by all; ask people, seek their thoughts.

From then on, the group will take overall control of the policy and ensure it is up to date. In addition, every quarter, they will have an external e-mail audit done, to measure how effective the policy is. The use of an external auditor is key to unbiased reporting on the policy in place, and it will provide critical information on information flowing in and out of the company, pornographic, sexist or defamatory remarks which can be embedded inside spreadsheets.

It is absolutely critical that for the first two audits people are told they will take place. I am a huge believer in personal freedoms, but that is very different from personal licence. We can call it Big Brother if we wish, we can complain about lack of trust, but ultimately we have to appreciate, and take personal responsibility for, the consequences of our actions.

So, next time you press F5, or send, just check it through, once again, because when it disappears into the ether, it stays there forever…

Many e-mails pass comment on other people and departments inside the same organisation. Santa Claus forwarded

*me this one and asked me to include it in the book. I am
delighted to do so:*

Dear Father Christmas,
I hope this e-mail finds you, and finds you well.

*It is difficult to believe it is that time of year again. That
wonderful season of goodwill, when we decorate our
desks, go wild at our office parties and are really kind to
each other, just for once.*

*I have been asked to write to you, and nominate
presents for myself and my fellow board members. We
have all been very good this year (me especially) and so
fully deserve to receive all on this list on Christmas night.
I have written a short sentence about each of us, so you
can understand the roles we play in the organisation.*

Chief Executive Officer
(The man who thinks he runs the company.)

- *An A–Z of the company building as he does not
seem to be able to find his way outside of his own
office. Please send a paper version only.*
- *A joke book, to improve on his present attempts,
which are not only deadly boring, but make no sense
whatsoever. (That doesn't stop us laughing out of
politeness and career security, though.)*

Financial Director
*(The man who thinks he will run the company, after the
man who currently thinks he runs the company.)*

- *A copy of our annual report written in clear, plain
English so that we can all know what is really going*

on in the organisation!

- *A holiday voucher for the North Pole, that must be taken in September next year – to save the rest of us going through the annual budget hell.*

Sales and Marketing Director
(The woman who can't run the company, because she would sell it.)

- *A mobile phone – to enable her to at least phone the rest of us when she makes a sale, so we have some advance idea of what we have just sold.*
- *A pair of floating shoes, to enable her to do what she already believes she can, walk on water.*

HR Director
(The woman who knows who runs the company, but says it's strictly private and confidential.)

- *A paper shredder for all of the mind-numbing forms, documents and papers that are circulated every week.*
- *An automated Performance Related Pay scheme that calculates all of the salary increases on a completely random basis – just as we do at the moment, only faster and without hassle.*

IT Director
(The man who wants to run the company, but is a little too busy right now.)

- *Some pudding. After all, he had his first course (year 2000) which cost us a fortune, he had his second*

*course (dot com), which cost us even more. This guy
needs a next course to justify any money.*

● *A crystal ball – for seeing the future that he is supposed to know, predict and understand.*

*By the way, if you ever decide to make a career move,
please give me a call. You have all the characteristics we
are looking for in our company:*

1   *Project Management – The ability to plan, work and
    deliver on time, every year – I don't remember pres-
    ents not arriving on time, ever – well done!*

2   *No one sees you delivering – just like all of us feel
    every day!*

3   *You have to meet people's requirements, and expec-
    tations, no matter how unreasonable and expensive.*

*With very best wishes,
(Name and address supplied)*

If you wish to stay on Leadership of Company, go to **A
Leader's Biggest Timewasters** 4 (p49)
or
If you wish to change journey, join **Leadership of Teams**,
go to **Project Leadership** 43 (p273)

**Fast-Track guide to the seven journeys –
Chapter Numbers**

Self	16	22	29	30	47	2	8	42
People	3	49	36	40	10	7	20	42
Teams	27	15	35	43	28	37	45	42
Company	39	18	6	34	51	4	25	42
Culture	21	32	23	11	9	31	19	42
Skills	24	41	12	14	48	44	33	42
Career	50	5	17	13	38	26	46	42

index

**The
Children's
Society**

A Voluntary Society of The Church of England

Edward Rudolf House
Margery Street
London WC1X 0JL

T: (020) 7841 4400
F: (020) 7841 4500
www.childrenssociety.org.uk

Dear David

I write to thank both you and Transworld Publishers for supporting the Children's Society by donating such a generous proportion of revenue from the sales of "The Naked Leader."

It is both exciting and refreshing that the messages of empowering people, in our case children and young people, to realise their full potential is so complementary. We too believe it is everyone's birthright to be able to live a happy life, full of promise and opportunity.

Your book captures one of the many potential agendas and behaviours of the next business age. We see today's children as being critical in making that age a success, both for themselves as adults and for the children of that age.

If any readers are interested in finding out more about our work, please visit us at www.childrenssociety.org.uk.

With best wishes

Bob Reitemeier

Bob Reitemeier
Chief Executive
The Children's Society